Salmon

C O O K B O O K

by Carol Ann Shipman

hancock

house

ISBN 0-88839-515-9
ISBN 0-88839-583-3 (Alaskan edition)
Copyright © 2004 Carol Ann Shipman

Second printing 2005

Cataloging in Publication Data

Shipman, Carol Ann, 1944–
   Salmon cookbook / Carol Ann Shipman.

   (Nature's gourmet series)
   Includes index.
   ISBN 0-88839-515-9 — ISBN 0-88839-583-3 (Alaskan ed.)

   1. Cookery (Salmon)   I. Title.   II. Series.
TX748.S24S32 2004   641.6'92   C2003-910990-9

Printed in China—JADE

Editing: Nancy Miller
Series design and production: Nando DeGirolamo
Photographic sources listed on page 93.

Published simultaneously in Canada and the United States by

HANCOCK HOUSE PUBLISHERS LTD.
19313 Zero Avenue, Surrey, B.C. Canada, V3S 9R9
(604) 538-1114 Fax (604) 538-2262

HANCOCK HOUSE PUBLISHERS
1431 Harrison Avenue, Blaine, WA, USA, 98230-5005
(604) 538-1114 Fax (604) 538-2262
Web Site: www.hancockhouse.com *email:* sales@hancockhouse.com

dedication

This book is dedicated to my brother-in-law Arthur Post, the devoted salmon fisherman in the family.

acknowledgments

I was very fortunate to work with a wonderful team to produce this book. I appreciate and thank all the people who were involved, and give special thanks to my husband Richard Shipman, and my son Mark Loeppky for their constant support and understanding testing endless recipes for all of my cookbooks.

To my publisher David Hancock, who shared my vision for the series, thank you for your patience and enthusiasm for this book.

To Nando DeGirolamo, my designer and partner, for his outstanding design for the entire series, that makes this book on first printing a best seller.

I'm very fortunate to have wonderful friends such as Eva Toni, my long time friend, who has eaten and, I think, enjoyed so many of the dishes in this book.

Thank You!

contents

6 appetizers

16 soup & salad

breakfast & brunch 28

main course 44

condiments 84

cooking tips 89

appetizers

Quality wild salmon is easy to recognize. Here's what to look for: Fresh salmon never smells fishy, it smells...fresh. Fresh salmon flesh will give slightly when you press it with a finger, then spring back into shape.

Smoked Salmon Stuffed Cucumber Slices

SERVES 8 – 10

3	**medium cucumbers**	3
4 oz.	**cream cheese, salmon flavored** whipped	125 g
1/4 cup	**red sweet pepper** finely chopped	60 mL
1/2 tsp	**fresh dill**	2 mL
1/4 cup	**smoked salmon**	60 mL
6 tbsp	**Havarti cheese** shredded	90 mL

Peel cucumbers, if desired. Cut cucumbers into 1/2-inch slices. With a small spoon scoop out most of the seeds from the cucumber slices without going through the other side. Place slices upside down on paper towels and drain for 5 minutes.

Combine filling of cream cheese, sweet pepper and dill; gently stir in Havarti cheese and salmon. Spoon filling into the indentation in each cucumber slice. Cover with plastic wrap and chill up to 12 hours.

Smoked Salmon and Chevre Cheesecake

SERVES 12

1-1/2 lbs	**goat cheese**	680 g
1/2 lb	**cream cheese**	227 g
1/2 cup	**sugar**	125 mL
12	**whole eggs**	12
4 cups	**sour cream**	1000 mL
1/4 cup	**lemon juice**	60 mL
2 cups	**smoked salmon** minced	500 mL
1/4 cup	**capers** small or coarsely chopped	60 mL
2 tbsp	**golden oregano**	30 mL
1 tbsp	**salt**	15 mL
1 tsp	**black pepper**	5 mL
	dash of Worcestershire sauce	
	dash of Tabasco	
1/4 lbs	**sweet butter**	113.5 g
1 cup	**chopped nuts**	250 mL

Preheat oven to 300°F (150°C). Cream goat cheese, cream cheese and sugar together. Incorporate eggs one at a time, blending constantly. Add sour cream, lemon juice, salmon, capers, oregano and seasonings. Let mixture rest in refrigerator for at least 1 hour to let flavors blend. Meanwhile, butter 8 3-ounce ramekins and coat with chopped nuts. Fill ramekins 3/4 full and bake in a water bath for approximately 2 hours. Chill in ramekins.

Salmon Wrap Appetizer

In large bowl, combine mustard, vinegar and dill weed. Add salmon strips and gently toss to coat. Refrigerate until ready to use. Defrost puff pastry sheets according to package directions. Unfold 1 pastry sheet and flatten gently, pressing seams. Cut into ten 1/2 inch strips. Cut each in half. (Repeat process with second pastry sheet after first one is used.) In small bowl, beat together egg and water; set aside.

Assemble using 1 strip of pastry, place a salmon strip in center crosswise. Brush each end of pastry strip with egg mixture. Fold over pastry around salmon. Place on greased cookie sheet. Repeat, making 40 appetizers. Brush tops of pastry with egg mixture. Bake in preheated 375°F (190°C) oven for 15 to 17 minutes until brown and puffy. Remove from cookie sheet and serve.

SERVES 15

1 lb	**salmon**	454g
	cut into 1/2-inch-thick slices, 2 inches long	
1/2 cup	**sweet-hot or honey mustard**	125 mL
2 tbsp	**rice wine vinegar**	30 mL
2 tsp	**dried dill weed**	10 mL
1	**medium package frozen puff pastry sheets**	1
2	**eggs**	2
1 tbsp	**water**	15 mL

Salmon Wrap Appetizer

Grilled Salmon Skewers with Gazpacho Salsa

Combine all marinade ingredients. Place in sealable plastic bag, add salmon. Refrigerate and allow to marinate for 1 hour.

In medium bowl combine all gazpacho salsa ingredients. Cover and refrigerate 1 hour to allow flavors to blend.

Remove salmon strips from marinade. Thread each strip onto a soaked skewer.

Grill Salmon
Oil grill. Over medium-hot coals or gas barbecue, grill salmon strips 4 minutes, turn and grill additional 3 minutes. Grill bread slices until toasted. Salmon will continue to cook after it is removed from grill. Salmon is done when meat flakes with a fork and is even in color. Place grill bread on each plate and top with salmon skewer. Spoon on gazpacho.

SERVES 4

1-1/4 lb	**salmon fillet** skin removed, sliced into 4 strips	567.5 g
4	**8-inch wooden skewers** soaked in water for 30 minutes	4
4	**1/2-inch-thick slices** **rosemary bread** brushed with olive oil	4

MARINADE

2 tbsp	**balsamic vinegar**	30 mL
1 tbsp	**olive oil**	15 mL
1 tbsp	**lemon peel** finely chopped	15 mL
1 tbsp	**fresh lemon juice**	15 mL
1	**garlic clove** finely chopped	1
1 tsp	**dry mustard**	5 mL
1 tsp	**salt**	5 mL
3/4 tsp	**ground black pepper**	4 mL

GAZPACHO SALSA

3/4 cup	**cubed red pepper**	175 mL
1/2 cup	**cucumber** peeled, seeded, cubed	125 mL
1/2 cup	**jicama** peeled, cubed	125 mL
1/4 cup	**red onion** finely chopped	60 mL
1/4 cup	**cilantro leaves** lightly packed and chopped	60 mL
2 tsp	**lemon peel** finely chopped	10 mL
1 tbsp	**balsamic vinegar**	15 mL
1 tbsp	**fresh lemon juice**	15 mL
1 tbsp	**fresh lime juice**	15 mL
1 tbsp	**honey**	15 mL
1/2 tsp	**salt**	2 mL
1/2 tsp	**black pepper** fresh ground	2 mL

Grilled Salmon Skewers with Gazpacho Salsa

Salmon in Silver Packets

SERVES 4

4	**3/4-inch-thick salmon steaks**	4
1/4 cup	**low sodium soy sauce**	60 mL
2 tbsp	**sherry or orange juice**	30 mL
1 tbsp	**dark brown sugar** packed	15 mL
2	**garlic cloves** finely chopped	2
1 tsp	**ginger root** finely chopped	5 mL
8-12	**drops red pepper sauce**	8-12
2 tbsp	**chopped fresh basil leaves**	30 mL
2 tbsp	**chopped fresh mint leaves**	30 mL
32	**thin bell pepper strips** about 2 bell peppers	32
2	**green onions** cut into 2-inch pieces and finely sliced lengthwise	2

Rinse and pat dry salmon steaks. Refrigerate until ready to use.

In medium bowl, combine soy sauce, sherry or orange juice, brown sugar, garlic, ginger and red pepper sauce; set aside. Combine basil and mint leaves; set aside.

To assemble foil packets, use a piece of aluminum foil that is 3 inches longer and 6 inches wider than salmon steak. Place steak in center of foil. Sprinkle with 1 tablespoon (15 mL) basil and mint leaves. Layer 8 bell pepper strips and one-quarter of green onions. Spoon on 1-1/2 tablespoons (22.5 mL) sauce.

To wrap, bring together long sides of foil over salmon and fold over several times. Fold ends of packet in several times to make snug packet. Repeat, making 4 packets.

Grill
Place foil packets on grill over moderate coals. Grill for 4 minutes per side. Let stand for 5 minutes. Open and serve.

Bake
Place foil packets on baking sheet and bake in preheated 400°F (205°C) oven for 15 minutes. Let stand for 5 minutes. Open and serve.

7 Gables Inn Broccoli Salmon Quiche

Preheat oven to 350°F (175°C). Prepare bottom of 9-inch (22 x 5 cm) pie dish by coating with nonstick cooking spray. Line with pie pastry. Cover bottom of dish with broccoli florets and chunks of salmon; sprinkle with cheese and chives, then set aside. In medium bowl, beat eggs, whipping cream, cayenne and dill until thoroughly combined; gently pour into pastry. Bake in preheated oven for 1 hour, or until crust and eggs are lightly browned and quiche is puffy in center.

SERVES 4

1	**9-inch pie crust**	1
2 cups	**fresh broccoli** cut in florets	500 mL
2 cups	**leftover cooked salmon, or canned**	500 mL
1 cup	**Swiss cheese** shredded	250 mL
1/4 cup	**fresh chives** chopped	60 mL
5	**eggs** beaten	5
1 cup	**whipping cream**	250 mL
1/4 tsp	**cayenne red pepper**	1 mL
1 tsp	**dried dill weed**	5 mL

"Kings" Salmon and Cognac Spread

YIELD 2 3/4 cups

4 oz	**salmon fillet**	125 g
1/3 cup	**white wine**	75 mL
1/2	**lemon** sliced	1/2
1	**minced shallot** divided	1
4 oz	**smoked salmon fillet**	125 g
8 oz	**cream cheese** softened	250 g
2 tbsp	**butter**	30 mL
1 tbsp	**whole grain mustard**	15 mL
1-1/2 oz	**cognac**	40 mL
1/2 tsp	**fresh ground pepper**	2 mL
1 tsp	**fresh dill** minced	5 mL
	garlic croutons	
	sliced cucumbers	

Rinse salmon fillet. In small pan, combine white wine, lemon and 1/2 chopped shallot; bring to a boil. Add salmon skin side up and reduce heat to simmer. Cook covered for 8 to 10 minutes. Remove salmon, and cool and strain poaching liquid. In food processor, blend together smoked salmon, cream cheese, butter and cognac just until smooth. Stir in mustard, pepper and dill. Flake poached salmon. Gently mix flaked salmon and poaching liquid into cream cheese mixture. Spoon into serving dish. Serve with garlic croutons and sliced cucumbers.

"Kings" Salmon and Cognac Spread

Kedron Valley Inn Smoked Salmon Parfait with Parmesan Toast

In a food processor, combine and puree salmon, egg whites, cream cheese and pepper. Slowly add heavy cream until firm consistency. Chill glasses. Remove salmon puree from processor and put in pastry bag with open tip. In chilled parfait glasses, layer 1 tablespoon (15 mL) onion, then approximately 2 oz (60 mL) of the salmon mousse, 1 tablespoon (15 mL) capers, more salmon mousse, 1/2 tablespoon (7.5 mL) parsley, more salmon mousse. Repeat for each glass.

Slice bread in thirds, lengthwise; bake at 400°F (200°C) for five minutes. Sprinkle Parmesan on each slice and bake again for another five minutes or until crisp. Slice and serve in parfait glass.

SERVES 8

16 oz	smoked salmon	454 g
2	egg whites	2
3/4 cup	whipping cream	175 mL
1-1/2 cups	soft cream cheese	375 mL
	white pepper to taste	
1 cup	red onion chopped	250 mL
1 cup	chopped capers	250 mL
1/2 cup	chopped parsley	125 mL
1	loaf French bread	1
1 cup	imported Parmesan cheese	250 mL
1 cup	white wine	250 mL

Smoked Salmon Roll Ups

Season the sour cream with salt and pepper, mustard and onion. Spread thinly on 2 x 3-inch slices of salmon. Roll up and fasten with toothpicks.

SERVES 4

1/2 lb	smoked salmon sliced	227 mL
1/2 cup	sour cream	125 mL
1/4 tsp	salt	1mL
1/4 tsp	freshly ground pepper	1 mL
1 tsp	prepared mustard	5 mL
1/2 tsp	minced onion	2 mL

soup & salad

Put some away! Well-wrapped salmon will freeze for up to two months in a refrigerator and three to four months in a deep-freeze. Using lined freezer paper, wrap tightly with at least two layers of paper from head to tail. Thaw slowly, unwrap, place in pan and cover, leave for 24 hours in the refrigerator.

Wildwood Herbed Baked Salmon on Rock Salt with Late Summer Tomato Salad

Wildwood Herbed Baked Salmon on Rock Salt with Late Summer Tomato Salad

Combine herbs and fennel seeds. Rub on flesh side of salmon fillets. Cover a large jellyroll pan with foil and pour in Kosher or rock salt to cover bottom of pan. Place salmon on salt, skin side down. Bake in preheated 325°F (160°C) oven for 35 to 45 minutes. Cooking salmon using this technique allows the salmon to be cooked through without becoming dry. The important factor is the low oven temperature. Remove salmon from oven and let stand for 5 minutes. To serve, use a wide knife or spatula to separate salmon from skin and portion onto plates. Spoon tomato salad around salmon and serve.

SERVES 4 – 6

1 cup	**fresh herb leaves** chopped fine, such as tarragon	250 mL
basil, Italian parsley and thyme		
2 tbsp	**fennel seeds** cracked	30 mL
4 lb	**salmon fillets** skin on	1816 g
2 lb	**kosher or rock salt** to cover bottom of pan	908 g
	tomato salad (recipe follows)	

Summer Tomato Salad

Combine all ingredients. Taste for seasonings. Let stand for 15 minutes. The salmon can be marinated overnight covered and refrigerated.

SERVES 4 – 6

4 cups	**cherry tomatoes** cut in half	1000 mL
1	**red onion** cut in half and sliced very thin	1
2	**cloves garlic** minced	2
1	**bunch whole basil leaves** chopped	1
1/2 cup	**extra virgin olive oil**	125 mL
1/3 cup	**balsamic vinegar**	75 mL
	salt and pepper to taste	

Café Valdez Classic Salmon Chowder

SERVES 4 – 6

4	**strips bacon** crumbled	4
6-8	**small red potatoes** quartered	6-8
1	**medium yellow onion** diced	1
3-4	**stalks of celery** chopped	3-4
1 cup	**chicken or vegetable broth** add more if needed	250 mL
2 cups	**sweet corn** drain if using canned	500 mL
2 tbsp	**Worcestershire sauce**	30 mL
2 tbsp	**fresh garlic** chopped	30 mL
1 tsp	**thyme**	5 mL
1 tsp	**pepper**	5 mL
1 tbsp	**fresh dill**	15 mL
1-1/2 lbs	**salmon fillets** remove skin, cut into small pieces about 1-inch square	680 g
1 cup	**whipping cream**	250 mL
	cooking sherry to taste	

Cook whole potatoes in pot until semi-firm and set aside. When cooled, cut into quarters. In a pot, cook bacon until crisp. Remove bacon, reserving drippings.

Sauté onions and celery in bacon fat. Add 1/2 cup (125 mL) of broth. Add potatoes, corn, dill, thyme, garlic, pepper and Worcestershire sauce. Cover and simmer for 10 minutes. Add salmon, cover and cook for 5 minutes.

Add whipping cream and stir at a low heat. Do not boil. Let rest for 10 minutes. Right before serving, add sherry and stir.

Garnish with crumbled bacon on top. Serve with a salad and warm bread.

Options: Add additional garlic. Corn can be left out. If a smoked salmon chowder is desired, use smoked salmon cut into small pieces and add at end with the cream.

Cream of Salmon Soup

SERVES 2 – 3

1 cup	**canned salmon**	250 mL
4 cups	**milk**	1000 mL
1	**slice of onion**	1
2 tbsp	**butter**	30 mL
2 tbsp	**flour**	30 mL
1/8 tsp	**pepper**	0.5 mL
1 tsp	**salt**	5 mL

Drain oil from salmon, remove skin and bones and rub through a coarse sieve. Heat milk and onion to scalding, remove onion. Melt butter, blend in flour, pepper, and salt; add milk gradually, stirring constantly. Add salmon and cook until smooth and slightly thickened. It is best to prepare the soup in a double boiler, but it can be made over direct heat if care is taken not to scorch or boil.

Salmon and Crab Bisque

Bring the water to a boil and add the whole crab, salmon bones and salmon. After 5 minutes remove the salmon and leave to cool. Simmer the crab and the bones for a further 15 minutes. In a separate pan, melt the butter and add the onion. When the onion has softened (4 or 5 minutes) add the flour and cook on a low heat for 2 minutes, then add the tomato puree. Start to add small quantities of the fish stock, stirring to keep smooth. Then bring to the boil and simmer for 20 minutes.

Meanwhile, remove the brown crabmeat and add to the soup. Flake the salmon and keep for garnish. Retain the white meat from the crab claws for garnish; the shell can be broken up and added to the soup at this stage for more flavor.

Strain the soup through a fine sieve and return to the stove. Add wine and leeks, simmer for 5 minutes and season with the ground pepper, salt and cayenne pepper. Add the cream and salmon garnish.

SERVES 4 – 6

1 lb	**whole crab** cleaned	454 g
1/2 cup	**salmon**	125 g
1 lb	**salmon bones**	454 g
4 cups	**water**	1000 mL
4 tbsp	**butter**	60 mL
4 tbsp	**flour**	60 mL
1/4 cup	**onion** finely chopped	60 mL
2 tbsp	**tomato puree**	30 mL
4 tbsp	**leek** finely chopped	60 mL
1/2 cup	**white wine**	125 mL
1/2 cup	**cream**	125 mL
	cayenne pepper	
	fresh ground black pepper	
	salt	

Salmon and Cucumber Salad

Cut cucumbers in half lengthwise; scoop out seeds and some flesh to form shell. Discard seeds; chop removed cucumber flesh into small pieces. Marinate in 1/4 cup (60 mL) of the French dressing for 1/2 hour. Drain salmon; reserve juice. Remove skin and bones; flake salmon into small pieces. Pour remaining French dressing over salmon; let marinate 1/2 hour in refrigerator.

SERVES 4

2	**cucumbers** washed	2
1/2 cup	**French dressing** divided	125 mL
1 cup	**canned salmon**	250 mL
1/3 cup	**thick mayonnaise**	75 mL
1 tbsp	**juice from salmon**	15 mL
	salt to taste	
	chopped parsley or chives for garnish	

Wildwood Wild Salmon Cakes

Wildwood Wild Salmon Cakes

In sauté pan, melt butter over low heat. Add shallots and cook for 2 minutes, being careful not to brown. In large bowl combine shallots, 1/2 cup (125 mL) breadcrumbs, cheese, lemon juice, mayonnaise, 1 beaten egg, mustard, bell pepper, parsley, salt and cayenne pepper. Gently mix salmon into mixture. Divide mixture into 12 equal portions and form into balls. Chill for 30 minutes in refrigerator. This can be done a day ahead, covered and refrigerated.

In small bowl, beat together remaining eggs and pour into shallow dish. Place flour and remaining 2 cups (500 mL) breadcrumbs in two separate shallow dishes. Remove salmon balls from refrigerator. Flatten each ball to make a 3/4-inch-thick cake. Dip each salmon cake in flour, then egg and breadcrumbs. In large skillet, heat 2 tablespoons (30 mL) oil over medium heat. Cook salmon cakes until golden brown, turn and brown other side, about 6 minutes total. Add more oil as needed during cooking process.

SERVES 12 – 18

1 tbsp	**unsalted butter**	15 mL
2	**shallots** finely chopped	2
2-1/2 cups	**homemade breadcrumbs** divided	625 mL
1/2 cup	**grated Asiago or Pecorino cheese**	125 mL
1/4 cup	**fresh lemon juice**	60 mL
1/4 cup	**mayonnaise**	60 mL
3	**large eggs** divided	3
2 tbsp	**Dijon mustard**	30 mL
2 tbsp	**green bell pepper** finely chopped	30 mL
2 tbsp	**fresh Italian parsley** chopped	30 mL
1 tsp	**salt**	5 mL
1/8 tsp	**cayenne pepper**	0.5 mL
1 lb	**cooked salmon fillets** bones, skin removed and flaked	454 g
1/2 cup	**flour**	125 mL
1/4 cup	**canola oil** divided	60 mL

Simple Salmon Salad

Drain fish; break into large pieces. Combine all ingredients except salad greens. Toss lightly; chill. Serve on salad greens.

SERVES 4

2 cups	**canned salmon**	500 ml
1 cup	**chopped celery**	250 ml
1/3 cup	**mayonnaise or salad dressing**	75 ml
2	**hard-cooked eggs** chopped	2
2 tbsp	**chopped onion**	30 ml
2 tbsp	**chopped sweet pickle**	30 ml
	salad greens	

Fresh Alaska Salmon and Italian Bread Salad

SERVES 4

2 cups	**stale Italian bread** cut into bite-size pieces	500 mL
1/2 cup	**white wine**	125 mL
1 tbsp	**olive oil**	15 mL
2	**garlic cloves** chopped	2
1 tbsp	**fresh basil** finely chopped	15 mL
1 tbsp	**fresh oregano** finely chopped	15 mL
1/8 tsp	**black pepper** freshly ground	0.5 mL
1 tbsp	**honey mustard**	15 mL
1 tbsp	**balsamic vinegar**	15 mL
1 lb	**Alaska salmon fillets** boneless	454 g
4 cups	**Romaine lettuce** chopped	1 kg
1-1/2 cups	**red pepper** diced	375 mL
3	**scallions** chopped	3
1 cup	**black olives** pitted and halved	250 mL
	freshly shaved Parmesan or Asiago cheese for garnish	

In a large, non-stick skillet, over medium-high heat, toast bread pieces for 5 to 6 minutes or until lightly toasted. Set aside.

In a small bowl, whisk together wine, olive oil, garlic, basil, oregano, black pepper, mustard and vinegar. Reserve 1/2 cup (125 mL) of this mixture for dressing. Pour remaining mixture in a large shallow bowl to marinate salmon fillets. Place fillets in marinade, turning the fish over to completely cover with the marinade. Leave fillets, skin side up, in the marinade for 15 minutes. Drain and discard marinade.

In the same skillet used for toasting the bread pieces, add salmon fillets skin side up and cook for 5 minutes over a medium-high heat. Turn carefully and cook for an additional 5–6 minutes on the other side. Remove from heat and cover. Let rest for 2 minutes or until the thickest part of the fillet is opaque and flakes easily with a fork. Place fillets on a cutting board and remove the skin. Cut into 4 equal portions.

While salmon is cooking, toss together the romaine, red bell pepper, scallions and olives. Divide among four plates. Place one-fourth of the bread chunks on each salad plate. Break each portion of salmon into large chunks, put on top of salad. Drizzle with reserved dressing and garnish with generous shavings of desired cheese.

Fresh Poached Salmon Salad with Fruit and Raspberry-Orange Vinaigrette

Rinse salmon fillets and set aside. In a medium skillet or fish poacher, bring to a boil the wine, clam juice, lemon and mint sprigs. Add salmon, skin side up, reduce heat to a simmer and cook covered 8 to 10 minutes or until cooked through. Remove salmon from poaching liquid. Cool to room temperature and remove skin. Arrange salad greens on each dinner plate. Arrange salmon, pineapple, raspberries and kiwi on greens. Drizzle with raspberry-orange vinaigrette and sprinkle with chopped cilantro.

Raspberry-Orange Vinaigrette
In small bowl, whisk together all ingredients. Refrigerate until ready to use.

Poached Salmon Salad with Fruit and Raspberry-Orange Vinaigrette

SERVES 4

4	**salmon fillets**	4
	6 oz (170 g)	
2 cups	**white wine or vegetable broth**	500 mL
2 cups	**clam juice**	500 mL
	(2-8 oz bottles) **or fish stock**	
1	**lemon**	1
	quartered	
2	**mint sprigs**	2
8 oz	**mixed salad greens**	250 g
2 cups	**fresh pineapple cubes**	500 mL
	well drained	
1-1/3 cups	**fresh raspberries**	325 mL
2	**kiwi**	2
	peeled and sliced	
1/3 cup	**chopped cilantro leaves for garnish**	75 mL

RASPBERRY-ORANGE VINAIGRETTE

1/2 cup	**raspberry vinegar**	125 mL
1/4 cup	**orange juice**	60 mL
3 tbsp	**olive oil**	45 mL
3 tbsp	**minced shallots**	45 mL
3 tbsp	**fresh mint leaves** chopped	45 mL
1 tbsp	**honey**	15 mL
1/2 tsp	**salt**	2 mL
1/8 tsp	**white pepper**	0.5 mL

Salmon Soup

SERVES 4

4	**salmon heads, backbones and tails** obtain these at fish store	4
3 cups	**water**	750 mL
2 tbsp	**olive oil**	30 mL
2	**large onions** finely chopped	2
6	**tomatoes** peeled, seeded and finely chopped	6
2	**juice and grated rind of two oranges**	2
4	**bay leaves**	4
	salt and pepper to taste	

Steam the salmon heads, tails and backbones for 4 minutes. Remove all meat and set aside. Place the bones and heads in a pan, adding the water. Boil stock with lid on for 1-1/2 hours.

In a separate pan, sauté the olive oil, onions, tomatoes, oranges and bay leaves until opaque. When boiled, remove the heads and bones from the stock. Strain into the tomato and onion mixture. Add fish, season and serve.

Loon River Café Salmon Stew

SERVES 6 – 8

2 tbsp	**butter**	30 mL
2 cups	**celery** finely chopped	500 mL
1	**cucumber** peeled, deseeded and diced	1
1 cup	**zucchini** diced	250 mL
2 lbs	**potatoes** diced	908 g
1/4 cup	**dry white wine**	60 mL
1 tbsp	**garlic** finely chopped	15 mL
4 tbsp	**fresh dill** finely chopped	60 mL
4 cups	**half & half cream**	1000 mL
1 cup	**clam broth**	250 mL
1 cup	**flour**	250 mL
1/4 cup	**oil**	60 mL
2 lbs	**salmon** diced	908 g
	salt and pepper to taste	

In a soup pan, melt the butter and sauté the celery, cucumber, zucchini and potatoes. When celery turns translucent, add wine and cook 2 minutes. Add clam broth. Add garlic, dill and cream. Simmer about 10 minutes. Thicken with 1/2 (125 mL) cup of roux (mix together 1 cup (250 mL) of flour and 1/4 cup (60 mL) oil), and then add salmon pieces. Simmer 20 minutes. Season to taste with salt and pepper. If it is too thick, add a little more water.

Loon River Café Salmon Stew

breakfast & brunch

Almost every cut of salmon is terrific over the coals. Be sure all grills are well oiled to ensure easy handling of salmon while barbecuing. Marinating and frequent basting will keep salmon moist and flavorful. If stuffing is used in the salmon, remember to measure salmon after it has been stuffed in order to calculate proper cooking time. Try cracker, cornmeal or cornflake crumbs for coating salmon. Add Parmesan cheese to crumbs for extra zest.

Abigail's Elegant Victorian Mansion Creamed Eggs with Smoked Salmon in Puff Pastry

SERVES 4

4	**puff pastry shells**	4
8	**large eggs**	8
2 tbsp	**butter**	30 mL
4-6 tbsp	**smoked salmon** chopped	60-90 mL
2 tbsp	**red peppers** chopped	30 mL
2 tbsp	**green peppers** chopped	30 mL
2 tbsp	**sour cream**	30 mL
1	**recipe of hollandaise sauce** *see* page 40	1
	parsley and paprika optional	

Bake 4 pastry shells according to package directions. Cool and prepare for serving. In pan, melt butter and add salmon and peppers; sauté until peppers are just barely limp. Add eggs, cook and stir until almost done, add sour cream and stir. Do not let eggs get too dry, remove from heat while still creamy.

Divide in 4 pastry shells, allowing some of the egg mixture to overflow on plate. Cover with 2 or 3 tablespoons (30–45 mL) hollandaise and sprinkle with parsley or paprika. Serve with fresh fruit in season; melon is excellent.

Blue Heron Glacier Bay Smoked Omelet

SERVES 3 – 4

1 tbsp	**melted butter**	15 mL
6	**eggs**	6
1/8 cup	**evaporated milk**	30 mL
	pinch of salt	
1 tbsp	**fresh chives** chopped	15 mL
	fresh pepper, to taste	
1/4 cup	**smoked salmon**	60 mL
	sautéed mushrooms and onions optional	
	sour cream and capers optional	

Beat eggs and milk until light. Heat butter in a skillet and pour in the egg mixture. Roll eggs around the pan and cook until it starts to set. Tip pan to the side and lift up the edges so the uncooked portion can slip under the set eggs. As eggs start to firm up, add the sautéed onion and mushrooms, chopped chives and crumbled smoked salmon. Fold over the egg mixture to have a proper 1/2 circle omelet. Serving your omelet with sour cream and chives is a nice choice. Portions vary, based on richness and amount of salmon used. Great served with sourdough bread, toasted.

Cascade View Bagels and Lox Benedict

Cut bagels in half and place cut side up on an 11 x 17 inch (28 x 43 cm) baking sheet. Bake at 450°F (230°C) oven for 5 to 8 minutes. Put 2 bagel halves on each plate and top equally with salmon and onion. Place a poached egg on each half, spoon sauce equally over portions, and garnish with dill.

Sauce

Using a 2–quart (2.25 L) pan, whisk broth and cornstarch until smooth. Stir over medium heat until boiling, about 2 to 3 minutes. Whisk in sour cream, lemon juice and capers. Stir frequently for 2 to 3 minutes and season with salt and pepper.

SERVES 6

6	**plain bagels**	6
1-1/4 cups	**smoked salmon** thinly sliced	310 mL
12	**slices red onion**	12
12	**poached eggs**	12

LIGHT LEMON CAPER SAUCE

1 cup	**chicken broth**	250 mL
2 tbsp	**cornstarch**	30 mL
1/4 cup	**sour cream**	60 mL
2 tbsp	**lemon juice**	30 mL
2 tbsp	**drained capers**	30 mL
	salt and pepper	

Casa de La Paz Bayfront Smoked Salmon Tart

Preheat oven to 375°F (190°C). Cut each piecrust into 16 circles using a 2-inch biscuit cutter. Place circles in greased miniature muffin cups. Using a whisk, mix cream with eggs in a large bowl. Stir in remaining ingredients. Spoon 1 tablespoon (15 mL) of filling into each shell. Bake for 25 minutes or until golden brown; cool. Remove from pans and store in a tightly covered container in refrigerator.

Tarts may be frozen. Thaw and then cover with aluminum foil and bake at 375°F (190°C) for 5 to 10 minutes.

YIELD 48 tarts

3	**9-inch refrigerated piecrusts**	3
1-1/2 cups	**half & half cream**	375 mL
4	**eggs**	4
1/4 lb	**smoked salmon** chopped	114 g
1/4 cup	**Monterey Jack cheese** shredded	60 mL
1/4 cup	**green onions** chopped	60 mL
1/2 tsp	**dried dill weed**	2 mL
1/4 tsp	**salt**	1 mL
1/8 tsp	**black pepper**	0.5 mL

The Mill House Inn Smoked Salmon and Cream Cheese Quesadillas

SERVES 6 – 8

3/4 cup	**low-fat cream cheese** softened	175 mL
2 tbsp	**fresh dill** chopped	30 mL
2 tsp	**fresh dill for garnish**	10 mL
1 tbsp	**fresh lemon juice**	15 mL
6	**8-inch flour tortillas**	6
	salt and pepper, to taste	
12 oz	**smoked salmon** sliced	375 g
3	**scallions** chopped, green parts only	3
1	**lemon** thinly sliced into rounds	1

In a bowl of an electric mixer, combine the cream cheese, 2 tablespoons (30 mL) of the dill, salt and pepper and lemon juice. Beat until smooth and well blended; set aside. In a large skillet, warm each tortilla over low heat until lightly browned on each side. Set aside on a cookie sheet.

For each quesadilla, spread about 2 tablespoons (30 mL) of the cream cheese mixture evenly on a tortilla, covering to the edges. Arrange 4 tablespoons (60 mL) of the sliced smoked salmon over the cheese. Repeat with the remaining tortillas stacking like pancakes. Sprinkle with the reserved 2 teaspoons (10 mL) of chopped dill. Cut tortilla stack into 6 wedges. Serve garnished with lemon slices and sprinkle with scallions.

1794 Watchtide by the Sea Smoked Salmon Claffouti

SERVES 2

1 tbsp	**melted butter**	15 mL
3	**Roma tomatoes** chopped	3
1/2 cup	**smoked salmon** flaked	125 mL
2	**scallions** chopped, green parts only	2
1 cup	**Jarlsberg cheese** grated	250 mL
4	**eggs**	4
1 cup	**milk**	250 mL
3/4 cup	**flour**	175 mL
1	**dash of English dry mustard**	1
1/4 tsp	**white pepper**	1 mL

Preheat oven to 350°F (175°C). Use large pie plate, shallow casserole dish or large iron skillet. Coat pan bottom with melted butter. Cover with chopped tomatoes, flaked salmon, scallions and cheese.

In blender, mix eggs, milk, flour, mustard and pepper. Blend until smooth. Pour over salmon mixture. Bake about 55 to 65 minutes or until custard is set to the point that a knife inserted comes out clean. Let sit 5 minutes before slicing.

Pasta with Asparagus and Smoked Salmon

Steam asparagus for 2 minutes and set aside. In a bowl, combine the mustard, wine and thyme. Melt the butter in a medium-sized pan over medium heat. Add the asparagus and smoked salmon; heat and stir for 1 minute. Season with pepper. Pour the mustard-wine sauce over the asparagus and salmon and simmer for 5 minutes. While the sauce is simmering, cook the pasta according to package directions. Drain well. Pour the sauce over the freshly cooked pasta, toss and serve immediately.

SERVES 4

1 lb	**asparagus** peeled, cut into 1-1/2-inch lengths, steamed	454 g
1/2 cup	**dry white wine**	125 mL
1/3 cup	**Dijon mustard**	75 mL
1 tsp	**dried thyme**	5 mL
2 tbsp	**butter**	30 mL
3/4 cup	**smoked salmon** cut into 1/2-inch-wide pieces	175 mL
3/4 lb	**fettuccine**	375 g
	lots of freshly ground black pepper	

The Seal Beach Inn Curry Salmon Quiche

Cut butter into flour. Add iced water 1 tablespoon (15 mL) at a time until dough is moist but not wet. Flour board and roll dough into desired shape. Press into pie plate and flute edges. Preheat oven to 425°F (220°C) degrees.

Filling

Sauté onions in a small amount of oil and set aside. Grate cheese and set aside. Beat eggs and cream, season with salt, pepper and curry. Drain salmon and take out bones. Chunk salmon, don't flake, and put in base of piecrust. Start building your quiche by placing onions on the bottom of the piecrust then egg-cream mixture. Top with grated cheese. Bake for 15 minutes at 425°F (220°C), reduce heat to 375°F (190°C) and continue to bake for 20–25 minutes or until mixture sets firmly.

SERVES 2

4	**eggs**	4
1-3/4 cups	**half & half cream**	425 mL
6	**green onions** chopped	6
1 cup	**grated cheese** any variety	250 mL
	salt and pepper, to taste	
2 cups	**canned pink salmon**	500 g
1 tsp	**curry powder**	5 mL
1	**pie crust** recipe follows	1

QUICHE PASTRY

1 cup	**flour**	250 mL
1/2 cup	**butter**	125 mL
3 tbsp	**cold water**	45 mL

Chili Grilled Salmon with Mango Salsa

Chili Grilled Salmon with Mango Salsa

Preheat barbecue to medium-high and oil the grill. Mix together all ingredients, except salmon, in a small bowl. Reserve 1 tablespoon (15 mL) of this mixture to season the salsa (see recipe below). Smear remaining mixture over the flesh side of the salmon.

Sear salmon, flesh side down for 3 minutes, turn over, cover grill and cook another 7 to 10 minutes until salmon just flakes when pressed with a fork. Alternatively, place salmon on grill skin side down and cook, covered, for 10 to 12 minutes. Serve with salsa drizzled on top or in a side dish.

SERVES 4

1-1/2 lbs	**salmon fillet** skin on	681 g
2 tbsp	**chili oil, or substitute olive oil plus hot pepper sauce to taste**	30 mL
2 tbsp	**lime juice**	30 mL
2 tbsp	**cilantro** finely chopped	30 mL
1 tbsp	**fresh ginger** grated	15 mL
2	**garlic cloves** minced	2

FRESH MANGO SALSA

1	**tomato** diced	1
1	**mango** peeled and diced	1
1/4 cup	**green onion** chopped	60 mL
2 tbsp	**cilantro** chopped	30 mL
1 tbsp	**reserved chili oil mixture**	15 mL
salt and ground pepper, to taste		
	Combine just before serving.	

Yoo-Sah or Sockeye Mulligan Stew

Place potatoes, water and salt in a large pot with a tight cover; bring to a boil over high heat. Boil potatoes for 5 minutes. Add carrots and onions, reduce heat and simmer partially covered for another 10 minutes until potatoes are just tender. Add salmon cubes, stir gently, scatter snow peas on top, cover and cook 5 minutes. Gently stir in seaweed and cilantro. Add salt and pepper to taste. Seaweed and cilantro can be found in your Oriental food section of most large supermarkets.

SERVES 4

3	**medium potatoes** peeled, cut into 1-inch cubes	3
4 cups	**cold water**	1 L
1/2 tsp	**salt**	2 mL
1 cup	**sliced carrots**	250 mL
1 cup	**red onion** chopped	250 mL
1-1/2 lbs	**sockeye fillet** skinned, cubed 1 inch	680 g
1 cup	**snow peas**	250 mL
1/2 cup	**dried seaweed** chopped	125 mL
1/4 cup	**fresh cilantro** chopped	60 mL

Flery Manor "Between the Sheets"

SERVES 4

1/2	**of a package Pepperidge Farm® puff pastry sheets**	280 g
6 tbsp	**butter**	90 mL
1 lb	**mushrooms** sliced	454 g
1 cup	**Champagne**	250 mL
2-1/4 cups	**white sauce mix**	560 mL
2 cups	**milk**	500 mL
4	**eggs**	4
1/2 cup	**sliced smoked salmon**	125 mL

Melt 4 tablespoons (60 mL) butter over medium-high heat in large skillet. Sauté mushrooms until they are limp and very little liquid remains. Add pepper to taste. Pour 1/2 (125 mL) cup of the Champagne over mushrooms and cook until liquid is reduced by 1/2 (about 2 to 3 minutes). Remove mushrooms with slotted spoon and reserve liquid (there should be about 1/4 (60 mL) cup of liquid).

Prepare puff pastry according to package for mini Napoleons, but cut each of the 3 strips into 2, not 4, rectangles. Split cooked pastries into 2 layers, making 12 layers in all. Prepare white sauce mix according to package directions, using the 2 cups (500 mL) of milk and the and 1/4 (60 mL) cup reserved liquid.

In a medium-sized skilled, melt the remaining 2 tablespoons (30 mL) butter and fry the 4 eggs until the whites of the eggs are set. Add remaining 1/2 (125 mL) of Champagne to skillet. Cover with lid and cook until eggs are firm (or to desired firmness).

Assemble: Place 1 pastry layer over each of the four plates, browned side down. Divide the mushrooms evenly over each, reserving some for garnish. Top with another layer of pastry, add egg to each and top egg with slices of smoked salmon, allowing the salmon to extend over the egg and out from under the next layer of pastry you are going to add. Place last layer on top. Pour sauce over top of each, garnish with mushrooms around the base, and top with a little caviar and parsley if desired. Serve immediately.

The Lilac Inn Smoked Salmon Quesadilla

Heat 2 tortillas on a dry skillet, turning often to prevent them from becoming hard. When both tortillas are warm, spread cream cheese on one side of each tortilla (this keeps the fillings from slipping out). Top the cream cheese with thinly sliced apples, onion and pieces of smoked salmon. Sandwich the two tortillas together. Slice in pie-shaped wedges.

SERVE 6

12	**flour tortillas**	12
1 lb	**cream cheese** room temperature	454 g
1 lb	**presliced smoked salmon**	454 g
3	**apples** thinly sliced	3
2	**red onions** sliced	2

The Apricot Cat BBQ Salmon Strata

Grease a 9 x 13 inch (22 x 33 cm) Pyrex dish. Make the sandwiches of cream cheese, dill, green onion and salmon. Depending on bread size, slice into quarters and lay in the dish. Beat together eggs, mustard, milk, salt and pepper; pour over top. Sprinkle with Swiss cheese and refrigerate overnight.

Remove from the refrigerator 1/2 hour before baking. Preheat oven to 325°F (160°C). Leave dish uncovered for 1/2 hour, and continue cooking for another 1/2 hour covered.

SERVES 4 – 6

6	**egg bread** large slices	6
1/4 cup	**Winnipeg style cream cheese** whipped	175 mL
1/2 lb	**BBQ salmon tips**	227 g
	fresh dill or dried, to taste	
2	**green onions** minced	2
4	**eggs**	4
2 tsp	**Dijon mustard**	10 mL
2 cups	**milk**	500 mL
	salt and pepper to taste	
1/2 cup	**Swiss cheese** grated	125 mL

French Scrambled Eggs with Smoked Salmon

SERVES 4

8	**large eggs**	8
1/4 lb	**unsalted butter** cut into pieces	113.5 g
1/2 tsp	**salt**	2 mL
1/2 tsp	**freshly ground pepper**	2 mL
2 tbsp	**whipping cream**	30 mL
8 oz	**smoked salmon** boned, skinned, julienned	250 g
1/2 cup	**Hollandaise sauce** see recipe on page 40 (packaged Hollandaise sauce mix can be used, follow package instructions)	125 mL
8	**smoked salmon** slices	8
2 tbsp	**chives** chopped	30 mL

Preheat broiler. Beat the eggs just until well mixed. Coat the bottom and sides of a saucepan with some of the butter. Add salt and pepper and 2 tablespoons (30 mL) of the butter to the eggs and put in the pan. Put the pan into a water bath of simmering water and stir the eggs with a wooden spoon, making sure to scrape all the surfaces of the pan, especially the corners. Never stop stirring or let the eggs stick to the pan. If the eggs start to thicken too quickly, remove the pan from the water for a minute or so. When the eggs are nearly done, stir in the cream and the julienned salmon.

Remove from heat, and stir in the remaining butter, which will halt the cooking as well as enrich the texture and taste of the eggs. Put the eggs on 4 warm ovenproof plates and spoon over equal amounts of the Hollandaise sauce. Broil for 1 minute to glaze the sauce. Place 2 slices of salmon on each plate and sprinkle with the chopped chives.

Old Town Inn Dilled Eggs with Smoked Salmon

SERVES 4

8	**eggs**	8
2 tbsp	**cold water**	30 mL
6	**drops hot sauce**	6
1/2 cup	**natural cream cheese**	125 g
1/4 cup	**smoked salmon**	60 mL
1 tsp	**fresh dill**	5 mL

Scramble eggs with water and hot sauce. Cut cream cheese into pieces. Dice salmon into half-inch thickness. Snip dill. Melt butter and scramble egg mixture. When eggs are no longer liquid, add cream cheese and salmon. Add dill at the end after eggs are cooked. Serve garnished with sprig of dill.

Abigail's Hotel Smoked Salmon Scrambled Eggs

Combine eggs, dill, salt and pepper. Melt butter in pan, add egg mixture and cook over low heat, gently stirring until just set. Add smoked salmon. Stir lightly.

Havarti Sauce

Heat saucepan, pour in oil and blend in flour until a roux is formed. Add stock, bring to simmer and add cheese and dill. Adjust seasonings with salt and pepper.

Place bottom half of bannock bun on a plate and spoon on egg mixture. Place top half of bannock just off center. Garnish with a sprig of fresh dill tucked under the top piece of bannock.

SERVES 4

12	**eggs** lightly beaten	12
1 tsp	**dill** omit if serving with Havarti sauce	5 mL
	salt and pepper to taste	
1/4 cup	**butter**	60 mL
1/2 cup	**smoked salmon** diced	125 mL
6	**bannock buns (or 8 bagels)** cut in half	6

HAVARTI SAUCE

1 cup	**chicken stock**	250 mL
1/2 cup	**Havarti cheese** grated	125 mL
1 tsp	**dill weed**	5 mL
1/2 cup	**vegetable oil**	125 mL
1/2 cup	**white flour**	125 mL

Market Sauté of Salmon

Heat a large, nonstick skillet over medium-high heat; add sun-dried tomatoes, oil and garlic; sauté for 1 minute. Add the mushrooms and asparagus and cook, stirring often, for 2 to 3 minutes. Add salmon, green onions; sauté another 5 to 7 minutes. Stir in parsley; add salt and pepper to taste. Serve over hot pasta.

SERVES 4 – 6

1-1/2 lbs	**salmon fillet** skinned, cut into 1-inch cubes	680 g
1/3 cup	**sun-dried tomatoes in oil** slivered	75 mL
1 tbsp	**oil from sun-dried tomatoes**	15 mL
2	**garlic cloves** minced	2
1 cup	**sliced mushrooms**	250 mL
1/2	**bunch of asparagus** cut into 1-inch pieces	1/2
1/2 cup	**green onion** sliced	125 mL
1/4 cup	**parsley** chopped	60 mL
	salt and ground pepper, to taste	
6 cups	**penne pasta** cooked	1500 mL

Smoked Salmon Wraps and Salad

SERVES 4

1 cup	**smoked salmon** sliced	250 mL
1/3 cup	**cream cheese**	75 mL
2 tsp	**fresh ginger** minced	10 mL
1 tsp	**lemon zest** minced	5 mL
1	**green onion** minced	1
1	**garlic clove** minced	1
	dash hot pepper sauce	
	salt and freshly ground pepper, to taste	
4	**flour tortillas** 8-inch (20-cm)	4
8	**whole butter lettuce leaves** washed	8

SALAD

3 tbsp	**rice wine vinegar**	45 mL
3 tbsp	**vegetable oil**	45 mL
2 tsp	**honey**	10 mL
1 tsp	**wasabi or mustard powder**	5 mL
	salt and freshly ground pepper, to taste	
8 cups	**salad greens** washed and chilled	2000 mL

In a small bowl, combine the cream cheese, ginger, lemon zest, green onion, garlic and hot pepper sauce. Add salt and pepper to taste. Spread each tortilla evenly with 1/4 of the cream cheese mixture, cover each with 2 lettuce leaves then 1/4 of the smoked salmon slice. Roll up tightly and place on a plate, seam down. Cover and chill for 1 hour.

Salad

Whisk together rice wine vinegar, vegetable oil, honey and wasabi. Add salt and pepper to taste. Just before serving, toss salad greens with dressing and divide among 4 plates. Trim ends of each wrap and slice diagonally into 8 pieces. Arrange wrap sections around outside edge of salads and serve.

Easy Hollandaise Sauce

YIELD 1 cup

1/2 cup	**butter**	125 mL
4	**egg yolks**	4
1/4 tsp	**salt**	1 mL
1/4 cup	**lemon juice**	60 mL
1/4 cup	**light cream**	60 mL

Heat the butter in double boiler until just melted. Add salt and lemon juice to egg yolks and mix well. Turn down heat so water is just simmering. Stir the egg mixture into the butter and beat with rotary beater until thick. Add the cream and beat 2 minutes more. This Hollandaise sauce will be paler in color than other Hollandaise recipes.

Smoked Salmon and Fennel Potato Pizza

Pour oil into a hot fry pan, add onions and fennel; sauté for 5 minutes. Season with salt and pepper, add wine, lower heat and simmer for 10 to 15 minutes until vegetables are tender and liquid has evaporated.

While fennel is cooking, grate potatoes onto a clean tea towel, roll towel up and squeeze grated potatoes dry, transfer to a bowl. Add chives, cornstarch, salt and pepper, toss well to mix.

Heat a second large fry pan over medium-high heat, add oil and then the potato mixture. Using a large spatula, press potatoes down to cover bottom of pan evenly, keep pressing down and cook for 5 to 6 minutes; carefully flip over and continue pressing and cooking for another 5 minutes until crusty and golden. Slide onto a platter, spread with the warm fennel, top with smoked salmon and chives. Drizzle with sour cream and finish with lots of freshly ground pepper. Serve immediately.

SERVES 4 – 6

2 tbsp	**olive oil**	30 mL
1	**medium onion**	1
2 cups	**fresh fennel bulb** finely chopped	500 mL
	salt and freshly ground pepper, to taste	
1/2 cup	**white wine**	125 mL
3	**medium potatoes** peeled	3
1/2 cup	**chives or green onions** minced	125 mL
1 tbsp	**cornstarch**	15 mL
	salt and pepper to taste	
2 tbsp	**olive oil**	30 mL
1/2 lb.	**smoked salmon** sliced	250 g
2 tbsp	**chives or green onions** minced	30 mL
3 tbsp	**sour cream** stirred	45 mL
	freshly ground pepper, to taste	

Mountain View Fatad with Smoked Salmon

Preheat oven to 375°F (190°C). In a bowl, combine eggs and ricotta cheese, salt and pepper. Pour 1/3 of egg mixture into a greased glass casserole dish. Layer with salmon and half the cheese, then top with remaining egg mixture. Cover with remaining cheese and sprinkle with oregano. Bake for 30 to 40 minutes or until skewer inserted in center comes out clean.

SERVES 4

9	**eggs**	9
2 cups	**ricotta cheese**	500 mL
	salt and pepper, to taste	
1/4 lb	**smoked salmon** sliced thin	113.5 g
1/4 lb	**mozzarella** grated and divided	113.5 g
2 tsp	**fresh oregano**	10 mL

Grilled Salmon Sandwich with Roasted Summer Vegetables

SERVES 4 – 6

1-1/4 lbs	**salmon fillets**	567.5 g
	skin removed, cut into four portions	

MARINADE

2 tbsp	**Worcestershire sauce**	30 mL
1 tbsp	**fresh lemon juice**	15 mL
1 tbsp	**fresh basil leaves** chopped	15 mL
1	**garlic clove** finely chopped	1
1/2 tsp	**ground black pepper**	2 mL
1/4 tsp	**salt**	1 mL
4	**slices rosemary bread** 1/2-inch-thick	4

ROASTED SUMMER VEGETABLES

1	**medium zucchini** sliced 1/4-inch thickness	1
2	**medium red onion** thinly sliced and made into rings	2
1	**leek** white part only, thinly sliced	1
1	**medium red bell pepper** seeded, sliced into 1/2-inch strips	1
1	**medium yellow bell pepper** seeded, cut into 1/2-inch strips	1
1	**Chinese eggplant** sliced into 1/4-inch thick strips	1
3 tbsp	**balsamic vinegar** divided	45 mL
1 tbsp	**olive oil**	15 mL
1	**garlic clove** finely chopped	1
1 tbsp	**rosemary leaves** chopped	15 mL
1 tsp	**ground black pepper**	5 mL
1/2 tsp	**salt**	2 mL

Marinade
In small bowl, combine marinade ingredients. Place fillets in sealable plastic bag. Add marinade, seal and turn bag to coat salmon with marinade. Refrigerate for 1 hour.

Oil grill. Cook salmon fillets over moderate coals, 4 inches from source of heat for 5 minutes, turn and cook additional 3 minutes. Grill bread. Let stand for 5 minutes.

Roasted Summer Vegetables
Combine all vegetables in large roasting pan. Combine 2 tbsp (30 mL) of the balsamic vinegar, oil, garlic, rosemary, pepper and salt. Pour over vegetables, tossing to coat. Roast in preheated 375°F (190°C) oven for 45 to 50 minutes, stirring every 15 minutes. Remove from oven; pour on remaining balsamic vinegar and toss. Serve roasted vegetables on top of grilled bread. Top with salmon fillet.

Grilled Salmon Sandwich with Roasted Summer Vegetables

The Painted Lady Smoked Salmon Roulade

Heat oven to 350°F (175°C). Line 9 x 13-inch (22 x 33 cm) pan with aluminum foil. Grease foil generously. Beat flour, milk, dill weed, butter, salt, eggs and onions until well blended. Pour into pan. Sprinkle with salmon. Bake uncovered for 15 to 18 minutes, or until eggs are set. Immediately sprinkle with cheese and spinach. Roll up, beginning at narrow end, using foil to lift and roll roulade. Cut into thick slices.

One cup (250 mL) of canned salmon, drained and flaked, may be substituted for the smoked salmon.

SERVES 8 – 9		
1/2 cup	**flour**	125 mL
1 cup	**milk**	250 mL
1 tbsp	**fresh dill weed** chopped or 1 tsp (5 mL) dried	15 mL
2 tbsp	**butter** melted	30 mL
1/4 tsp	**salt**	1 mL
4	**eggs**	4
3	**medium green onions** chopped	3
1 cup	**smoked salmon** flaked or chopped	250 mL
1-1/2 cups	**Gruyere or Swiss cheese** shredded	375 mL
1 cup	**fresh spinach** chopped	250 mL

main course

The secret to successful salmon cookery is Do Not Overcook! Whichever
cooking methods you choose, your salmon will be cooked to perfection when
the flesh becomes opaque, flakes readily, and is easily pierced with a fork.
Storing salmon is easy. Place the fish on a platter or pan with a double
layer of paper towels underneath. Put two or three slices of lemon on the
top of the fish, then dampen a tea-towel with tap water and lay over top.
Wrap the fish with cling-wrap and store on the bottom shelf of the
refrigerator. Salmon will store well this way for up to two days.

Cedar Plank Salmon

SERVES 4

1-1/2 lb	**salmon fillet**	680 g
1/4 cup	**olive oil**	60 mL
1	**lemon or orange** juice and zest	1
1 tbsp	**fresh basil** chopped	15 mL
1/2 tsp	**salt**	2 mL
1 tsp	**fresh ground black pepper**	5 mL

Marinate the salmon in remaining ingredients. Meanwhile, soak a piece of untreated cedar plank in cold water for about 2 hours (weighting it with something heavy), then place in a 450°F (230°C) heated oven for 5 to 10 minutes. Remove the salmon from the marinade and bake on the plank until cooked, allowing about 10 minutes per inch (2.5 cm) thickness of fish.

Barbecue
Soak the plank as above. Place salmon on plank. Put the plank directly on the barbecue grill. Close the lid and cook over medium-high heat for about 20 minutes.

Honey Bourbon Salmon

SERVES 2

1 lb	**salmon fillet**	454 g
MARINADE		
3/4 cup	**bourbon**	175 mL
2 tbsp	**honey**	30 mL
1/2 tsp	**ginger** minced	2 mL
1/2 cup	**brown sugar**	125 mL
2 tsp	**soy sauce**	10 mL
	pepper to taste	

Combine marinade ingredients and pour over salmon; marinate for 1 hour.

Preheat then oil grill rack. Grill salmon for 2–3 minutes on each side.

Creamy Royal Tasmanian Smoked Salmon & Pasta

SERVES 4

8 oz	**smoked salmon** sliced	250 g
1/4 cup	**black olives** chopped	60 mL
2 tbsp	**olive oil**	30 mL
1	**small onion** chopped	1
1 cup	**cream**	250 mL
	fresh basil leaves	
1 tbsp	**brandy**	15 mL
8 oz	**pasta**	250 g

Heat oil and sauté onion until soft. Add olives to pan with cream and brandy. Bring to boil and cook until thickened slightly. Chop basil and stir into cream. Cut smoked salmon slices into strips and fold into cream. Cook pasta and drain. Pour sauce over the top of pasta and serve.

Cedar Plank Salmon

Gold Medal Grilled Tequila Salmon

SERVES 6 – 8

2 lbs	**salmon fillets**	908 g
2 tbsp	**butter**	30 mL
1	**lime zest and slices for garnish**	1

LIME TEQUILA MARINADE

1/2 cup	**olive oil**	125 mL
6 tbsp	**lime juice**	90 mL
6 tbsp	**Tequila**	90 mL
2	**jalapeño peppers** minced	2
2 tbsp	**lime zest**	30 mL
1 tsp	**chili powder**	5 mL
2 tsp	**sugar**	10 mL
1 tsp	**coarse salt**	5 mL

Mix marinade ingredients in bowl; let stand 15 minutes or longer. Marinate salmon in mixture for 1 to 2 hours in refrigerator.

Drain marinade and set aside. Place salmon steaks, skin side down, on a large piece of greased foil. Place over low heat on barbecue, with lid closed for 10 minutes. Brush generously with marinade. Close lid again and turn heat to medium. Grill about 8 minutes longer. Do not overcook. Meanwhile, boil remaining marinade in heavy saucepan about 5 minutes. Whisk in butter. Drizzle over grilled salmon. Garnish with lime zest and lime slices.

Crystal Palace Poached Salmon

SERVES 1

1	**salmon fillet**	1
1	**orange**	1
2 tbsp	**olive oil**	30 mL
	crushed black pepper	
	dash of ginger powder	
	fresh parsley, to taste	
1/2 cup	**fish stock**	125 mL
1/2 cup	**white cooking wine**	125 mL
1	**garlic clove** finely chopped	1
2 tbsp	**butter**	30 mL

Cut 2 slices of orange and squeeze the rest of the orange on top of the fish. Add olive oil, crushed pepper and ginger powder. Let the fish marinate for 15 minutes. While the fish is marinating, turn on a burner to medium heat and put 1/2 cup (125 mL) of fish stock in a pan and add wine. Bring the mixture to a boil. Reduce the heat to a simmer. Add the marinated fish and put the 2 orange slices on top of the fish. Cover pan with a lid. Simmer until the fish is done. Remove fish to a platter, leaving the liquid in the pan. Reduce the liquid by boiling it to half and then add butter. Stir and pour over fish.

Mahogany Glazed Salmon

In a small saucepan, whisk together chicken broth, soy sauce, brown sugar, ginger, cornstarch, orange juice and peel. Bring to a boil over medium heat and cook 5 minutes, stirring often. Pour glaze into a 9 x 13 inch (22 x 33 cm) Pyrex pan and let cool 20 minutes.

Place fillets skin side up in glaze, cover and refrigerate for 1 to 8 hours. Preheat barbecue to medium-high and oil the grill. Remove fillets from glaze and place on grill skin side up. Sear salmon for 2 minutes, turn over, cover and cook another 7 to 10 minutes until salmon just flakes when pressed with a fork. Alternatively, place salmon on grill skin side down and cook, covered, for 10 to 12 minutes. Be careful as glaze burns easily. Pour remaining glaze into a small saucepan and boil 1 minute over medium-high heat. Serve salmon with the hot glaze.

SERVES 6

6	**salmon fillets** skin on, 6-oz (175-g)	6
1	**can chicken broth** (10 oz/284 mL)	1
1/2 cup	**soy sauce**	125 mL
1/3 cup	**packed brown sugar**	75 mL
1 tbsp	**fresh ginger** grated	15 mL
1 tbsp	**cornstarch**	15 mL
1	**orange** juice and peel only	1

Peking Salmon

Place the salmon steaks in a Pyrex baking dish. Whisk together the mustard, soy sauce, orange juice and oil in a bowl. Pour the sauce over the salmon steaks and marinade for 2 to 3 hours. When ready to serve, place the salmon under a hot grill. Baste with the marinade, and grill for 4 minutes per side. Transfer to a platter and serve.

SERVES 4 – 6

4	**salmon steaks** 3/4-inch thick	4
2 tbsp	**soy sauce**	30 mL
2 tbsp	**oil**	30 mL
1/4 cup	**hot mustard**	60 mL
2 tbsp	**orange juice**	30 mL

Honey Lime BBQ Kebobs

Honey Lime BBQ Kebobs

Place salmon and vegetables into a large flat dish. In a small bowl, whisk together the lime juice and zest, soy sauce, honey and garlic, until honey is dissolved; pour over salmon and vegetables. Season with salt and pepper, toss everything gently together, cover and refrigerate for 6 hours.

Preheat barbecue to medium-high and oil the grill. Alternate the marinated salmon and vegetables onto the soaked skewers.

In a small bowl, whisk together the lime juice and honey. Place skewers on hot grill and cook ten minutes, basting often with honey mixture and turning once.

SERVES 6 – 8

3 lbs	**salmon fillet** skin on, cut into 1-inch chunks	1362 g
1	**green pepper** cut into 1-inch squares	1
1	**red onion** cut into 1-inch squares	1
2 cups	**mushrooms** halved	500 mL
1	**lime, juice and zest**	1
1/2 cup	**light soy sauce**	125 mL
1/4 cup	**creamed honey**	60 mL
2	**garlic cloves** minced	2
	salt and fresh ground **pepper, to taste**	
12-16	**long bamboo skewers** soaked overnight	12-16
2	**limes** juice	2

Salmon with Crab Sauce

Season salmon with 1 teaspoon (5 mL) of the lemon pepper, set aside. Melt butter in a saucepan over medium-low heat. Stir in the flour and let cook, bubbling gently, for 1 minute. Gradually whisk in milk and add remaining lemon pepper. Cook, stirring often, until sauce has thickened, about 12 minutes.

Remove sauce from heat. Whisk in cream cheese until melted. Stir in lemon juice, peel, green onions and crab (with juices if using tinned). Keep sauce warm over very low heat, stirring occasionally. Broil or pan-fry seasoned salmon for 3 to 5 minutes per side until salmon just flakes when pressed with a fork. To barbecue, place salmon skin side down on an oiled grill and cook covered for 10 minutes or until salmon just flakes when pressed with a fork. Top with crab sauce.

SERVES 4

1-3/4 lbs	**salmon fillets** skin on, cut into 4	795 g
2 tsp	**lemon pepper** divided	10 mL
2 tbsp	**butter**	30 mL
2 tbsp	**flour**	30 mL
2 cups	**whole milk**	500 mL
1/2 cup	**light cream cheese** cubed	125 g
1	**lemon** juice and peel only	1
1	**green onion** thinly sliced	1
1/4 lb	**fresh crabmeat**	135 g

Seared Salmon with Caramelized Onions

Heat 2 tablespoons (30 mL) of butter in pan and sear salmon over a high heat, keeping the fish slightly undercooked, 3 minutes each side. Remove from pan and keep warm. Melt the remainder of butter in same pan, add the ginger, dill and onion and cook until darkened. Add soy sauce, red wine vinegar and white wine, cooking for 5 minutes to give a thick onion mixture. Return salmon to pan and heat through. Serve salmon with onion on top and juices around the edge of the plate.

SERVES 4

4	**3-oz (85-g) portions of salmon** skin on	4
4 tbsp	**butter** divided	60 mL
1	**small onion** thinly sliced	1
1/4 tsp	**ginger** chopped	1 mL
1/2 cup	**white wine**	125 mL
1 tsp	**red wine vinegar**	5 mL
1/4 cup	**fresh dill** chopped	60 mL
1 tsp	**soy sauce**	5 mL

Salmon Steaks with Spinach Pesto

SERVES 4		
4	**salmon steaks**	4

SPINACH PESTO SAUCE		
1/4 cup	**pine nuts**	60 mL
1 cup	**olive oil**	250 mL
2 cups	**fresh spinach leaves** lightly packed	500 mL
1 cup	**fresh basil leaves** lightly packed	250 mL
1 cup	**Parmesan cheese** grated	250 mL
3	**small garlic cloves**	3
1/2 tsp	**coarse salt**	2 mL
1/4 tsp	**pepper**	1 mL

Lightly grill salmon steaks until just cooked. Salmon will continue cooking after removing from heat. Drizzle spinach pesto sauce over salmon steak before serving.

Spinach Pesto Sauce

Toast pine nuts in heavy skillet over medium-high heat until pale golden brown, stirring constantly, about 4 minutes. Transfer nuts to processor. Add olive oil, and remaining ingredients. Blend until nuts, spinach, basil and garlic are finely ground, adding more oil if necessary to obtain texture of soft mayonnaise, about 2 minutes. Heat and drizzle over cooked salmon.

Hartness House Hazelnut Braised Salmon

SERVES 4		
4	**8 oz salmon fillets**	4
2 cups	**hazelnuts** finely chopped	500 mL
1/4 cup	**butter**	60 mL
1/2 cup	**water**	125 mL
1 tbsp	**shallots** chopped	15 mL
1/2 cup	**Frangelico liqueur**	125 mL
2 cups	**whipping cream**	500 mL
	salt and pepper, to taste	

Press the salmon fillets into the hazelnuts, lightly coating the fish. Preheat a sauté pan with butter and sear the salmon on both sides, about 30 seconds each, or until light brown. Transfer to a baking dish and add water. Bake in a 350°F (175°C) oven for 10 to 15 minutes or until the salmon is firm to the touch.

In a saucepan, reduce the shallots and liqueur by half. Add whipping cream and reduce by half again, stirring continuously. Continue to reduce until the sauce begins to thicken. Add salt and pepper to taste. Ladle 4 tablespoons (60 mL) of sauce on each serving plate; place a salmon fillet on the sauce and serve.

Salmon Steaks with Spinach Pesto

Roasted Salmon Mediterranean

SERVES 4		
4	**6-8 oz (175-225 g)** **salmon fillets** skin on	4
1 tbsp	**olive oil**	15 mL
1 tbsp	**fresh lemon juice**	15 mL
1 tbsp	**fresh rosemary** chopped	15 mL
freshly ground pepper, to taste		
1 tsp	**olive oil**	5 mL
salt to taste		

Pat salmon dry with paper towel. Whisk together the oil, lemon juice, rosemary and pepper. Rub onto salmon, covering all sides, place on a plate, cover loosely and marinate in refrigerator for 1 hour.

Preheat oven to 425°F (220°C). Using an ovenproof nonstick skillet, brush skillet with olive oil and preheat on stovetop. Remove salmon from fridge and season with salt. Place salmon flesh side down in very hot skillet to sear for 1 minute. Turn salmon. Immediately place hot pan with salmon into the hot oven and roast for 8 minutes. Test for doneness. Salmon should flake easily when pressed with a fork.

My Sister Louise's Teriyaki Salmon Steaks

SERVES 2		
2	**salmon steaks**	2
1 tbsp	**butter or margarine**	15 mL
1 tbsp	**parsley flakes**	15 mL
1 tbsp	**lemon juice**	15 mL
1 tsp	**ginger** minced	5 mL
1 tsp	**garlic** minced	5 mL
few drops of teriyaki sauce		
salt and pepper, to taste		

Place butter in nonstick frying pan and melt over medium-low heat. Add minced ginger, garlic, parsley flakes and lemon juice. Mix well. Increase heat, being careful not to burn the butter. Add salmon steaks and cook. Add salt and pepper to taste. More butter and lemon juice can be added if needed.

Just before salmon steaks are completely cooked, add a few drops of teriyaki sauce. Turn salmon steaks to coat each side with the sauce. Serve with lemon slices and fresh parsley.

Excellent served with brown rice and green vegetables.

Inn at Portsmouth Harbor Corn Cakes with Smoked Salmon and Crème Fraiche

In a large bowl, pour the boiling water over the cornmeal. Add the butter and set aside while the butter melts. In another bowl, blend flour, baking powder and sugar. In a smaller bowl, beat eggs well then add milk, scallions and corn. When the cornmeal is cool, add the egg mixture and stir with a spatula until smooth. Add dry ingredients and blend well.

To make the sauce, blend the sour cream with the red onion and wine. Refrigerate until ready to use.

Heat a griddle over medium heat and lightly grease with a few drops of vegetable oil. Heat oven to 200°F (95°C). Drop 1/3 cup (75 mL) of batter onto griddle. When bubbles appear, flip and brown lightly on other side. Place on baking sheet in oven to keep warm while cooking remaining corn cakes.

Serve, placing 3 cakes on each plate with rolled salmon slices and a dollop of crème in the center. Sprinkle with scallions or chives.

The batter can be made the night before and refrigerate, as can the crème fraiche. These cakes are also delicious served with sliced grilled ham and maple syrup!

SERVES 6

1 cup	**boiling water**	250 mL
1 cup	**yellow cornmeal**	250 mL
4 tbsp	**butter** cut into small pieces	60 mL
1 cup	**unbleached white flour**	250 mL
1-1/2 tsp	**baking powder**	7.5 mL
3 tbsp	**sugar**	45 mL
3	**extra large eggs**	3
1 cup	**milk**	250 mL
4	**scallions** thinly sliced	4
1 cup	**corn kernels** If using frozen, defrost and drain well	250 mL
1/3 lb	**smoked salmon** thinly sliced	152 g
	vegetable oil for griddle	

CRÈME FRAICHE

3/4 cup	**nonfat sour cream**	175 mL
2 tbsp	**red onion** finely chopped	30 mL
1/3 cup	**dry white wine**	75 mL

Salmon with Basil and Champagne Cream Sauce

SERVES 4

2 tbsp	**butter**	30 mL
1/4 cup	**chopped shallots**	60 mL
2 cups	**dry Champagne or sparkling wine**	500 mL
2 cups	**whipping cream**	500 mL
1 cup	**pine nuts** toasted	250 mL
1 cup	**packed fresh basil**	250 mL
2 tbsp	**olive oil**	30 mL
4	**8-oz (250-g) salmon fillets** 3/4-inch thickness	4
	olive oil	
1/2 cup	**chives or green onions** chopped	125 mL

Melt butter in heavy large skillet over medium heat. Add shallots and green onions sauté for 5 minutes. Add Champagne and boil until liquid is reduced to about 1/2 cup (125 mL). Add cream and bring to a slow boil until thickened to sauce consistency, stirring occasionally. Season to taste with salt and pepper. Set aside.

Blend pine nuts, basil leaves and 2 tablesoons (30 mL) oil in processor until finely chopped Season with salt and pepper. Preheat broiler, brush salmon with oil. Broil 3 minutes. Turn fish over and broil until cooked through. Remove from broiler, sprinkle pine nut mixture over salmon, pressing gently to adhere. Bring cream sauce to simmer and add chives. Spoon sauce over salmon.

Salmon Steaks with Vermouth

SERVES 4

4	**salmon steaks**	4
2 tbs[	**butter**	30 g
2 tbsp	**dry vermouth**	30 mL
1/2 cup	**double cream** whipping cream	120 g
1/2	**lemon, zest**	1/2
	salt and pepper	
	dill for garnish	

Melt the butter in a sauté pan. Add the salmon steaks and cook over a high heat; remove and keep warm. Add the vermouth, lemon zest and cream to the pan; season and boil until the sauce thickens slightly. Pour sauce over salmon and garnish with dill sprig. Serve with boiled potatoes and French beans.

Lemon Grass and Apricot Stuffed BBQ Salmon

Beat all stuffing ingredients together until well blended. Spoon butter onto a sheet of waxed paper and roll it up to 1 inch (2.5 cm) in diameter. Twist the ends closed and refrigerate until firm, about 1 hour.

Lemon grass is available fresh or dried (use half the amount of dried).

Sauté the onion and garlic in the butter for 2 to 3 minutes; add the mushrooms and cook another 5 minutes. Add lemon grass, apricots, rice, cayenne, salt and pepper to the mushroom mixture. Stir and cook another minute. Remove from heat and cool.

Stuff the salmon and close with skewers. Place the salmon in a barbecue fish holder or wrap in chicken wire (or aluminum foil). Brush salmon with olive oil. Place the salmon on the hot grill, cover and cook for 12 to 15 minutes, turn fish over and cook covered for another 10 to 15 minutes or until flesh is opaque and is just beginning to flake. Remove and let stand for 5 minutes. Top each serving with butter mix cut into "coins".

SERVES 6 – 8

2 tbsp	**butter**	30 mL
1	**small onion** finely chopped	1
1	**garlic clove** minced	1
1/4 cup	**mushrooms** finely chopped	60 mL
2 tbsp	**fresh lemon grass** finely chopped, inner stalks	30 mL
1/4 cup	**dried apricots** chopped	60 mL
1 cup	**cooked rice, preferably basmati**	250 mL
1/4 tsp	**cayenne powder**	1 mL
	salt and pepper, to taste	
3-4 lbs	**whole salmon** dressed	1362 g-1816 g
1 tbsp	**olive oil**	15 mL

STUFFING

1/4 cup	**unsalted butter** softened	60 mL
2 tbsp	**inner stalks of lemon grass** chopped	30 mL
1 tbsp	**lemon juice**	15 mL
	salt and pepper, to taste	

Ginger-Sesame Salmon

Arrange cooked hot salmon in a single layer on a serving platter. Stir together the soy sauce, seasoned rice vinegar and ginger and spoon over salmon. Cut green onions into 1-inch lengths then slice each piece into very thin strips; scatter over salmon. In a small skillet combine garlic and sesame oil. Warm mixture, stirring, over medium heat until garlic turns golden. Immediately drizzle oil mixture over salmon. Enjoy!

SERVES 4

1 1/2 lbs	**salmon** hot grilled, baked or broiled	681 g
2 tsp	**soy sauce**	10 mL
2 tsp	**seasoned rice vinegar**	10 mL
1 tbsp	**fresh ginger** minced or grated	15 mL
2	**green onions** ends trimmed	2
1	**garlic clove** minced or pressed	1
1 tbsp	**Oriental sesame oil**	15 mL

Asian-style Steamed Salmon

Asian-style Steamed Salmon

In a small bowl combine soy sauce, water, sesame oil, garlic, ginger, sugar and hot sauce; set aside. Place salmon fillets on an oiled rack, skin side down, over 1 to 2 inches of rapidly boiling water. Cover with a tight-fitting lid and steam for 8 to 10 minutes while keeping water at a constant boil. Remove cooked fillets to a platter and keep warm.

Steam spinach for 2 to 3 minutes and drain off excess liquid, if necessary.

Arrange spinach on individual warmed plates, top each with a piece of salmon and a little of the reserved sauce. Serve with any extra sauce and rice or noodles.

SERVES 4

4	**6 oz (175 g) salmon fillets** skin on	4
2 tbsp	**soy sauce**	30 mL
2 tbsp	**water**	30 mL
2 tsp	**sesame oil**	10 mL
1	**garlic clove** minced	1
1 tsp	**fresh ginger** minced	5 mL
2 tsp	**sugar**	10 mL
	dash hot pepper sauce	
2	**bunches spinach** washed and stemmed	2

Mahogany Manor Golden Baked Salmon

Place fish in ovenproof baking dish. Sprinkle with salt and spread with mayonnaise like you are frosting a cake. Sealing it to the bottom enhances the flavor as it keeps the salmon moist. Top with onion, tomato and cheddar cheese. Add paprika or pepper. Bake at 375°F (190°C) for 45 minutes. Add small amount of water to dish if necessary. I have done this with 8–10 pounds of fresh salmon by increasing the amount of mayonnaise to cover the fish and seal it to the dish. Bake it just a little longer. Any type of fish can be substituted for salmon.

SERVES 6

1 lb	**salmon**	454 g
1/3 cup	**mayonnaise**	75 mL
1/2 tsp	**salt**	2 mL
1	**medium onion** sliced	1
1/2 cup	**cheddar cheese** grated	125 mL
1	**tomato** sliced	1
	dash paprika or black pepper	

Roasted Spicy Salmon

Roasted Spicy Salmon

SERVES 6

3-4 lbs	**whole salmon** dressed	1362 g- 1816 g
1	**bunch cilantro** chopped	1
1/4 cup	**parsley** chopped	60 mL
2 tbsp	**mint leaves** chopped	30 mL
2	**jalapeño peppers** seeds removed	2
1 tbsp	**fresh ginger** minced	15 mL
2	**garlic cloves** minced	2
2 tbsp	**fresh lemon juice**	30 mL
2 tbsp	**vegetable oil**	30 mL
2 tsp	**cumin seeds** toasted	10 mL
1 tsp	**salt**	5 mL
1/2 cup	**tomato** diced	125 mL

Cut diagonal slashes about 4 inches long, 1-1/2 inches apart and 1/2-inch deep on each side of salmon. In bowl or food processor place cilantro, parsley, mint, peppers, ginger, garlic, lemon juice, vegetable oil, cumin and salt; pulse to make paste. Transfer to a small bowl and fold in tomato. Stuff spice mixture into slits and belly cavity of the fish. Cover and refrigerate 1 to 4 hours.

Preheat oven to 425°F (220°C). Transfer salmon to a lightly oiled roasting pan. For cooking time, measure the thickest part of the salmon and allow 10 minutes per inch of thickness. Or cook until fish flakes easily along both sides of backbone at thickest point when tested with a fork.

Smoke! Fire! Ice! Salmon Steaks

Line a wok or stockpot with foil. On top of the foil place the molasses, brown sugar, tea leaves, anise and coriander. Place a rack over the mixture and lay the steaks in a single layer on the rack. Cover the pot and cook over medium heat for 10 minutes. Remove pot from the heat and let stand for 10 minutes. Remove the salmon steaks from the pot and set aside.

Blanch the bean sprouts, red pepper, carrot and snow peas together for 2 minutes in boiling water. Drain well and place in a bowl; add the onion to this mix. Combine the vinegar, chili garlic sauce and oil; add to the vegetables and toss to coat

In a small bowl, combine the mayonnaise, grated ginger root and teriyaki; set aside.

Place the salmon steaks on a serving platter; surround with the vegetables, then top the salmon steaks with the mayonnaise mixture and garnish with the cilantro springs.

SERVES 4

2	**8-oz (250-g) salmon steaks** 1-inch thick	2
1/4 cup	**molasses**	60 mL
1/4 cup	**brown sugar**	60 mL
1/4 cup	**black tea leaves**	60 mL
1 tsp	**anise seed**	5 mL
1 tbsp	**coriander seed**	15 mL
1 cup	**bean sprouts**	250 mL
1	**small red pepper** julienned	1
1	**small carrot** julienned	1
1/4 lb	**snow peas**	135 g
1	**green onion** sliced	1
2 tbsp	**rice wine vinegar**	30 mL
2 tsp	**chili garlic sauce**	10 mL
1 tsp	**sesame oil**	5 mL
1/4 cup	**mayonnaise**	60 mL
1 tsp	**ginger root** grated	5 mL
1 tsp	**teriyaki marinade/sauce**	5 mL
	cilantro sprigs for garnish	

Salmon Steaks with Dill Butter

Lay each salmon steak on a piece of foil or baking parchment large enough to wrap it up. Mix together the herbs and butter and spread over the pieces of fish. Season with salt and pepper. Tip to pour the wine over the salmon and quickly close the foil or parchment to make a parcel. Bake in a preheated oven at 425°F (220°C) for 12 to 15 minutes.

SERVES 2

2	**salmon steaks** about 1-inch thick	2
2 tbsp	**chopped fresh dill**	30 mL
4 tbsp	**softened butter**	60 mL
4 tbsp	**dry white wine**	60 mL
	salt and pepper, to taste	

Salmon with Fresh Vegetables and Herbs

SERVES 4

4	**6 oz (175 g)** **fresh salmon fillets**	4

BALSAMIC MARINADE

1/3 cup	**olive oil**	75 mL
3 tbsp	**balsamic vinegar**	45 mL
3 tbsp	**seasoned rice** **wine vinegar**	45 mL
1 tbsp	**Dijon mustard**	15 mL
2	**garlic cloves** crushed	2
1/2 tsp	**salt**	2 mL
1/4 tsp	**coarsely ground** **black pepper**	1 mL
1/4 tsp	**crushed red pepper**	1 mL

VEGETABLES

4 cups	**broccoli florets** with 2-1/2 inch stems	1000 mL
1 cup	**Roma tomatoes** 1/2-inch dice	250 mL
1/3 cup	**red onion** diced	75 mL
2 tbsp	**capers**	30 mL
2 tbsp	**fresh basil** chopped	30 mL

Rinse salmon fillets, pat dry and set aside. In small bowl, whisk together oil, vinegar, mustard, garlic, salt, black and red peppers. Remove 1/4 cup (60 mL) marinade to baste salmon while grilling or broiling.

Steam broccoli about 5 to 8 minutes or until crisp-tender. Rinse with cold water. Place in large bowl with tomatoes, onion, capers, basil and dill. Pour remainder of marinade over the vegetables in bowl and marinate for about 1 hour. Grill or broil salmon and serve fish over room-temperature vegetables.

Grill salmon
Place a lightly oiled heavy-duty piece of aluminum foil just large enough to fit all of the salmon on grill. Poke several holes in foil. Arrange salmon fillets, skin side down on foil. Cover and grill over medium-hot coals. Do not turn.

Broil
Lightly oil broiler pan. Place salmon fillets, skin side down, on pan. Broil 4 inches from source of heat. Do not turn.

To determine cooking time, measure salmon at thickest part. For 1/2 to 3/4-inch salmon, cook 5 to 8 minutes total. For 1 to 1-1/2-inch salmon, cook 8 to 12 minutes total.

Salmon with Fresh Vegetables and Herbs

Minted Salmon and Asparagus Stir Fry

In a small bowl whisk together the fish sauce, oyster sauce, water, sugar and chili; set aside. Heat the oil over medium-high heat in a wok or large skillet. Place salmon in hot oil and sprinkle with garlic; cook 1 minute, turn and cook 2 more minutes. Add the cut asparagus and the reserved sauce mixture; bring to a boil, cover, reduce heat to medium and simmer for 3 to 5 minutes until salmon just flakes and asparagus is crisp-tender. Stir in mint and serve.

Asian fish sauce and oyster sauce are available in the oriental food section of most large supermarkets.

SERVES 4

1-1/4 lbs	**salmon fillet** skin on, cut in 4	700 g
2 tbsp	**Asian fish sauce**	30 mL
2 tbsp	**oyster sauce**	30 mL
2 tbsp	**water**	30 mL
2 tsp	**brown sugar**	10 mL
1	**fresh red chili** seeded, minced	1
2 tbsp	**olive oil**	30 mL
2	**garlic cloves** minced	2
1	**bunch thin asparagus** cut into 1-inch pieces	1
1/2 cup	**fresh mint** chopped	125 mL

Ranchero Grilled Salmon Steak with Roasted Corn-Black Bean Salsa

SERVES 4

4	**8-oz (250-g) salmon steaks**	4

CITRUS MARINADE

1/2 cup	**fresh orange juice**	125 mL
1/4 cup	**fresh lime juice**	60 mL
2 tbsp	**olive oil**	30 mL
2	**cloves garlic** crushed	2
1	**Serrano pepper** seeded and minced	1
2 tsp	**grated lime zest**	10 mL
1/2 tsp	**salt**	2 mL
1/8 tsp	**coarsely ground pepper**	0.5 mL

ROASTED CORN-BLACK BEAN SALSA

3-4	**ears fresh corn on the cob** husked and rinsed	3-4
1-3/4 cups	**canned black beans** rinsed well, drained	425 mL
1 cup	**diced Roma tomatoes** 1/3-inch dice	250 mL
1/3 cup	**green onion** minced including tops	75 mL
1/3 cup	**cilantro leaves** chopped	75 mL
2	**Serrano peppers** seeded and minced	2
1/2 tsp	**salt**	2 mL
1/2 tsp	**chili powder**	2 mL
1/4 tsp	**coarsely ground pepper**	1 mL
1/3 cup	**reserved citrus marinade**	75 mL

Rinse salmon steaks and pat dry. In small bowl, whisk together orange juice, lime juice, oil, garlic, Serrano pepper, lime zest, salt and pepper.

Remove 1/3 cup (75 mL) and reserve to add to salsa. Pour remainder of marinade over salmon in plastic bag, marinate in refrigerator while making salsa.

Place salmon on oiled grill, 4 inches from medium-hot coals. Grill salmon about 5 minutes on each side, brushing with marinade from time to time. Now discard leftover marinade. Salmon is done when meat flakes easily and is evenly colored. The salmon will continue to cook after it is removed from the grill. Serve salmon with Roasted Corn-Black Bean Salsa.

Roasted Corn-Black Bean Salsa

Roast corn on the barbecue until cooked and golden brown, about 5 to 10 minutes. Cool. Slice kernels off cob, about 1-1/2 cups (375 mL), and place in medium bowl with black beans, tomatoes, onion, cilantro, chilis, salt, chili powder, pepper and reserved marinade. Mix gently. Serve salsa over grilled salmon.

Ranchero Grilled Salmon Steak with Roasted Corn-Black Bean Salsa

Mediterranean Salmon

Combine all ingredients for the Olive Saltza in a small bowl; set aside.

Preheat oven to 425°F (220°C).

Place two grape leaves on work surface, overlapping each other. Place a salmon fillet in the center of the grape leaves with 1 oz (30 g) of the Olive Saltza, 1 oz (30 g) goat cheese and one lemon round. Wrap the grape leaves around the entire portion. Place each portion on a parchment paper square, on the lower third of the paper. Fold the outside edges of the parchment paper over the salmon. Fold the lower edges in and roll into a package. Repeat the process with remaining salmon fillets. Place packages on a cookie sheet and bake for 20 minutes. Unwrap and serve immediately with a rice dish.

SERVES 6

6- 8oz	**salmon fillets**	6-250 g
12	**grape leaves**	12
1 cup	**Olive Saltza** recipe follows	250 mL
6	**1-oz (30-g) goat cheese portions**	6
1	**lemon** sliced into rounds	1
6	**pieces parchment paper** 18 x 18 inch each	6

OLIVE SALTZA

1 cup	**assorted olives** pitted and chopped	250 mL
1 tbsp	**capers**	15 mL
3	**shallots** peeled, finely chopped	3
1	**medium red onion** peeled, finely chopped	1
1	**juice of a lemon**	1
1/4 cup	**extra virgin olive oil**	60 mL
3 tbsp	**good quality red wine vinegar**	45 mL

Salmon with Lime Yogurt Sauce

SERVES 4

4	**4-oz (125-g) salmon fillets**	4
2 tbsp	**fresh parsley** minced	30 mL
2 tbsp	**fresh basil** minced	30 mL
2 tbsp	**fresh chives** minced	30 mL
1 tsp	**fresh thyme** minced	5 mL
	vegetable oil	
1 cup	**onion** minced	250 mL
1	**bunch spinach** stemmed	1
1	**medium tomato** chopped	1
1	**garlic clove** minced	1

SAUCE		
1/2 cup	**plain yogurt**	125 mL
1 1/2 tsp	**fresh chives** chopped	7 mL
1/2 tsp	**fresh parsley** chopped	2 mL
1/2 tsp	**lime peel** minced, green part	2 mL
1/2 tsp	**fresh lime juice**	2 mL
	pepper to taste	

Sauce
Combine all ingredients in bowl. Season with pepper.

Prepare the barbecue or preheat broiler. Combine herbs in shallow dish. Coat skillet lightly with vegetable oil; heat skillet to medium heat. Add onion and sauté until tender. Add spinach, tomato and garlic. Sauté until spinach wilts, about five minutes. Set aside.

Grill or broil salmon until cooked through, about three minutes on each side. Coat salmon with herb mixture. Reheat spinach mixture. Serve salmon with spinach and sauce.

Zesty Salmon Steaks

SERVES 4

4	**salmon steaks** 1-inch thick	4
	pinch cayenne for each steak	
2	**garlic cloves** crushed	2
2 tbsp	**olive oil**	30 mL
1/3 cup	**fresh parsley or dill** chopped	75 mL
1 tsp	**capers**	5 mL
1 tsp	**lemon zest**	5 mL
1/4 cup	**lemon juice**	60 mL

Sprinkle each steak with cayenne. Sauté 1 clove of garlic in oil at medium heat until golden; remove clove from oil. Increase heat to medium-high. Sauté salmon 4 minutes each side. Add remaining garlic clove, parsley, capers, lemon zest and lemon juice. Cook 1 to 2 minutes longer. Serve steaks drizzled with pan juices.

Broiled Salmon with Ginger Butter

Broiled Salmon with Ginger Butter

Brush the steaks with oil and season with salt and pepper. Place under a broiler, 4 inches from the heat source, and broil 4 minutes per side. Serve with a dollop of ginger butter crowning each portion.

Cream together the ingredients for ginger butter until well mixed. Pack the flavored butter into a small crock and refrigerate until needed (the butter may be prepared several days in advance).

SERVES 6

2	**salmon steaks** 3/4-inch thick	2
2 tbsp	**vegetable oil**	30 mL
	salt and pepper, to taste	

GINGER BUTTER

6 tbsp	**butter** room temperature	90 mL
4 tbsp	**ginger preserves**	60 mL
1 tsp	**lime peel** finely grated	5 mL
1 tbsp	**chives** snipped	15 mL

The 1785 Inn Smoked Salmon Ravioli

SERVES 8

2 cups	**flour**	500 mL
2	**eggs**	2
2	**egg yolks**	2
1	**egg** beaten with 1/2 tsp (2mL) water	1

SMOKED SALMON MOUSSE

1 lb	**smoked salmon**	454 g
2	**eggs**	2
1 cup	**whipping cream** chilled	250 mL
1/2 tsp	**coarse ground pepper**	2 mL
2 tbsp	**chives** chopped	30 mL

SAUCE

1 lb	**Gruyere cheese**	454 g
1 cup	**whipping cream**	250 mL

To make the pasta, place the flour in a mound on a smooth work area, creating a well in the center. Pour the beaten eggs and yolks into the well and slowly pull the flour into the eggs until it is all incorporated. Finish kneading by hand, adding more flour if needed for a smooth consistency. Divide the pasta in half and roll out each half or feed through pasta roller until thin. Lay out the pasta on a smooth, floured surface.

For the mousse, mix the smoked salmon and eggs in a blender or food processor until smooth. Add the whipping cream in a slow stream along with pepper and chives and mix until well combined.

Divide the smoked salmon mousse into 24 equal-sized portions and place these portions two inches apart on one sheet of pasta. Brush egg wash on the pasta between the mounds of salmon mousse and cover with the other sheet of pasta. Cut raviolis apart and refrigerate or freeze until you are ready to use. Bring large pot of lightly salted water to a boil, add raviolis and cook about 6 minutes. At the same time add to each of 8 fireproof plates 1-ounce (28 g) gruyere cheese and 1/8 cup or about (30 mL) of cream. Heat under the broiler until the cheese melts, add three raviolis to each plate, and sprinkle with additional Gruyere cheese on top. Place this under a broiler until the cheese browns lightly.

Chef June's Salmon Guadalupe

Dip salmon in Cajun seasoning. Sauté salmon in a very hot pan with 1 tablespoon (15 mL) of the olive oil, for about 4 minutes each side.

Corn Cakes
Roast corn on grill, cut off the cob and place into bowl. Add the egg, butter, cornmeal, honey, cilantro and salt and pepper. Beat the ingredients with a wire whisk. Heat a non-stick skillet with remaining olive oil. Place corn cake batter in skillet and cook on each side for three minutes.

Julienne all fruit and place in bowl. Add the white wine, remaining honey, ginger, lemon juice, salt and pepper and blend well. Place some of the fruit slaw on the plate with corn cake and salmon, top with the crabmeat.

SERVES 1

1	8 oz salmon fillet	250 g
1 tbsp	Cajun seasoning	15 mL
2 tbsp	extra virgin olive oil	30 mL

CORN CAKE

1	corn on the cob roasted on grill	1
1	whole egg	1
2 tbsp	salted butter	30 mL
4 tbsp	yellow cornmeal	60 mL
2 tbsp	fresh cilantro	30 mL
1 tbsp	honey	15 mL
	salt and pepper to taste	

JICAMA SLAW

1 piece	jicama	1 piece
1	plum	1
1	cantaloupe	1
1	honeydew	1
1	mango	1
1	papaya	1
2 tbsp	white wine	30 mL
1 tbsp	lemon juice	15 mL
1 tsp	fresh ginger	5 mL
1 tbsp	honey	15 mL
2 tbsp	jumbo lump crabmeat	30 mL
	salt and pepper, to taste	

Southwest Chili Salmon

Mix all of the ingredients together, except salmon. Southwest Dry Chili Rub will keep indefinitely, stored in an airtight container. You will want to keep this rub on hand for all your seafood.

SERVES 6 – 8

6 -8	salmon steaks	6-8

SOUTHWEST DRY CHILI RUB

3 tbsp	medium chili powder	45 mL
1-1/2 tbsp	brown sugar	22.5 mL
2 tsp	garlic granulated	10 mL
2 tsp	paprika	10 mL
2 tsp	salt	10 mL
2 tsp	cumin, ground	10 mL
1 tsp	black pepper	5 mL
1 tsp	whole leaf oregano dried	5 mL
1/4 tsp	cinnamon	1 mL

*Salmon Fillets with
Country Herb Crust*

Salmon Fillets with Country Herb Crust

SERVES 4

4	**6 oz (170 g) salmon fillets** skin removed	4
1/2 cup	**almonds** toasted	125 mL
1 tbsp	**chilled butter** cut into small cubes	15 mL
2 tsp	**fresh herb leaves** finely chopped such as basil, oregano, dill, parsley	10 mL
1 tsp	**seasoned salt**	5 mL
1 tsp	**seasoned pepper**	5 mL

In food processor, coarsely chop nuts. Add butter, herbs, seasoned salt and pepper. Process until well mixed and mixture forms a ball, set aside. Rinse salmon fillets, pat dry. Lightly grease a baking pan. Place fillets on pan. Divide nut mixture evenly and spread, covering the top of each fillet. Bake in preheated 400°F (200°C) oven for 12 to 15 minutes or until salmon is done.

Salmon is done when meat flakes easily and is evenly colored. It will continue to cook for a few minutes after it is removed from the oven.

Seasoned salt and seasoned pepper can be purchased at your local supermarket.

Umberto's "Salmone Fresco Marinato"

This dish is cured rather than cooked, so use top-quality ingredients. In any cured or raw salmon dish, fresh wild salmon should first be frozen for 48 hours then thawed; alternatively, purchase previously frozen wild salmon.

Rinse salmon fillets with cold water and pat dry with paper towel. Mix the salt, peppercorns and sugar in a bowl. Rub this mixture into the salmon. Then rub the salmon fillets with the gin and olive oil.

Line a cookie sheet with a large piece of foil. Place one fillet skin side down on foil and cover top with fresh dill. Place the other fillet on top of the first, flesh side down. Top with another sheet of foil. Fold up foil to enclose salmon tightly. Place another cookie sheet on top and weigh it down with several large cans of tomatoes or other weights equaling about 10 lbs. Refrigerate for 48 hours, turning foil package every 8 to 12 hours. Remove from refrigerator, remove weights, place fillets skin side down on cutting board and slice very thinly on the bias. Garnish with lemon and dill. Left-over salmon may be kept refrigerated for up to 5 days.

SERVES 8 – 10

2-1 lb	**fresh salmon fillets** skin on	2-454 g
2 tbsp	**coarse salt**	30 mL
1 tbsp	**white peppercorns** crushed	15 mL
2 tbsp	**sugar**	30 mL
1 tbsp	**gin**	15 mL
2 tbsp	**olive oil**	30 mL
1	**bunch fresh dill**	1
	lemon wedges	
	dill sprigs	

Vermouth Salmon

Heat large fry pan over medium heat, add butter; add garlic, teriyali and vermouth to melted butter. Stir until mixed and flavors are well blended. Dredge salmon fillets in flour and add to pan. Cover and cook 5 minutes per side. Remove from heat, let sit in covered pan for another five minutes.

SERVES 4

4	**salmon fillets** skin removed	4
6 tbsp	**butter**	90 mL
1 cup	**flour**	
6 tbsp	**teriyaki sauce**	90 mL
4 tbsp	**dry vermouth**	60 mL
4	**garlic cloves** minced	4

SERVES 2 – 3

1 cup	**canned salmon** drained	250 mL
1 tbsp	**butter**	15 mL
1-1/2 tsp	**olive oil**	7 mL
1	**garlic clove** sliced	1
1	**small bulb fennel** sliced	1
1	**small red pepper** cut into chunks	1
4	**small tomatoes** cut into quarters	4
2	**green onions** sliced	2
30	**spinach leaves**	30
	salt and ground black pepper, to taste	

Braised Salmon and Fennel

Melt butter and olive oil together in a saucepan over medium heat. Put sliced garlic and fennel in the pan. Soften for 30 seconds. Add red pepper and tomatoes. Cover, lower heat and simmer for 10 minutes. Remove from heat. Add green onions, spinach and chunks of salmon. Put back on burner, cover and heat thoroughly for about 1 to 2 minutes. Add salt and pepper to taste.

The Eighteenth Street Inn Rubbed and Roasted Salmon

SERVES 2

1	**salmon side fillet**	1
RUB		
1 tbsp	**chili powder**	15 mL
1 tbsp	**brown sugar**	15 mL
1 tbsp	**white sugar**	15 mL
1 tbsp	**garlic powder**	15 mL
1 tsp	**cayenne pepper**	5 mL
1 tsp	**kosher salt**	5 mL
1 tsp	**cinnamon**	5 mL
1 tsp	**ground thyme**	5 mL
1 tsp	**cardamom**	5 mL
1 tsp	**onion powder**	5 mL
1 tsp	**black pepper** freshly ground	5 mL

Mix all seasoning ingredients together. Rub mixture over salmon (flesh side only) and let marinate about 30 minutes. Prepare a very hot grill or heat oven to 400°F (200°C). Lay fish over grill and cover. Do not touch until salmon releases itself from grill (it will break if you try to move it too early). If oven roasting, line a heavy baking sheet with foil and roast until flaky. Remove from grill to serving platter. Serve as an entrée or on crackers as an appetizer.

Lime Grilled Salmon Steaks with Tomato Avocado Salsa

Marinate salmon steaks in lime zest, lime juice, olive oil and jalapeno pepper in a shallow glass bowl at room temperature for 30 minutes or in the refrigerator for 1 hour.

Prepare the barbecue and oil the grill. Place the steaks on the grill at medium heat (or place under the broiler) and cook, turning once and basting with marinade for 4 to 5 minutes per side or until the salmon flakes easily.

Lime Grilled Salmon Steaks with Tomato Avocado Salsa

SERVES 4

4	**salmon steaks** 1-inch (2.5-cm) thick	4
1 tsp	**grated lime zest**	5 mL
1/4 cup	**fresh lime juice**	60 mL
1 tbsp	**olive oil**	15 mL
1 tsp	**fresh jalapeño** minced	5 mL

TOMATO AVOCADO SALSA
Combine salsa ingredients just before serving.

1	**tomato** diced	1
1	**ripe avocado** peeled and diced	1
2 tbsp	**fresh lime juice**	30 mL
1/4 cup	**red onion** minced	60 mL
1 tsp	**fresh jalapeño pepper** minced	5 mL
2 tbsp	**fresh cilantro** chopped	30 mL
salt and ground pepper, to taste		

Alaskan Sockeye Salmon Strudel

SERVES 4

1 lb	**sockeye fillets** cut in 1/2-inch strips	454 g
1/2 cup	**sour cream**	125 mL
3 tbsp	**oil-packed sun-dried tomatoes** drained	45 mL
1	**garlic clove**	1
1 tbsp	**oregano leaves** fresh	15 mL
	salt and pepper, to taste	
1/4 cup	**butter**	60 mL
2 tbsp	**fresh herbs** chives, parsley, thyme minced, mix together before measuring	30 mL
6	**phyllo leaves (sheets)**	6
3 tbsp	**prepared basil pesto**	45 mL

Place sour cream, sun-dried tomatoes, garlic, oregano, salt and pepper in food processor. Process until smooth and tomatoes, garlic and oregano are well incorporated. Melt butter and add minced herbs. On a sheet of parchment or waxed paper, place 1 phyllo leaf, with widest side facing you. Brush with herbed butter to cover entire surface. Repeat with remaining phyllo leaves.

Spread sour cream/tomato mixture over phyllo, lay salmon strips on top of mixture, overlapping as necessary to ensure even thickness of salmon. Rub top of salmon with pesto sauce to coat evenly. Fold edge closest to you over the salmon. Using the parchment paper, continue to roll the salmon into a strudel "log" until phyllo is gone. Fold ends under. Carefully place the strudel on parchment lined baking tray. Refrigerate for at least 1/2 an hour. This step is very important to assure flaky layers. Preheat oven to 400°F (205°C). Bake strudel until golden brown and then cut into 4 equal slices.

Barbecued Salmon Burgers

SERVES 4

1 lb	**salmon** boneless, skinless, well chopped	454 g
2 tbsp	**bread crumbs**	30 mL
1 tbsp	**Dijon mustard**	15 mL
1 tbsp	**onion** minced	15 mL
2 tsp	**lemon juice**	10 mL
1/2 tsp	**garlic** minced or pressed	2 mL
1/2 tsp	**black pepper** freshly ground	2 mL
1/2 tsp	**salt or to taste**	2 mL

Thoroughly combine the burger ingredients in a medium bowl.

Divide into equal portions, make into patties. Cook on the barbecue grill. The salmon patties are fragile, so handle them carefully; if you chill the patties on a plate in the refrigerator before putting them on the grill, they will hold together better.

Maple Mango-Tango Salmon

In a bowl, mix together chopped mango, 4 tablespoons (60 mL) maple syrup, coriander seed, green onions, rice vinegar, Tabasco sauce and garlic, set aside.

Measure out 1 cup (250 mL) of this mixture and place in a blender or food processor along with remaining 2 tablespoons (30 mL) maple syrup and process until pureed and smooth. Pour over fillet in a shallow glass dish and refrigerate for at least one hour.

To remaining mango mixture, add chopped bell red peppers to prepared maple mango salsa. Refrigerate.

Spray grill with nonstick vegetable spray and heat to medium. Place fillet on grill, 5 inches above heat, and grill 10 minutes per inch of thickness, measured at the thickest part, or until salmon just flakes when tested with a fork. Remove to serving platter and garnish with lettuce leaves. Spoon maple mango salsa over grilled salmon.

SERVES 4

1-1/2 lbs	**Alaska salmon fillets**	681 g
6	**fresh mangoes** peeled, chopped in 1/2-inch pieces	6
6 tbsp	**real maple syrup** divided	90 mL
1 tsp	**coriander seed** crushed	5 mL
1/4 cup	**green onions** chopped	60 mL
2 tsp	**rice vinegar**	10 mL
1/2 tsp	**Tabasco sauce**	2.5 mL
1 tsp	**minced garlic** **in a jar**	5 mL
1/3 cup	**red bell peppers** chopped	75 mL
1 tbsp	**fresh cilantro** chopped	15 mL
	Romaine lettuce leaves **for garnish**	

Honey Mustard Basil Salmon

Place salmon steaks in shallow baking dish. In a small bowl, mix together olive oil, lemon juice, mustard, honey and garlic. Stir in basil. Season with salt and pepper to taste. Spread mixture over steaks. Place on a plate, cover loosely and marinate refrigerated for 1 hour. Bake at 375°F (190°C) for 12 minutes or until salmon just flakes when pressed with a fork.

SERVES 4

4	**salmon steaks** 1-inch thickness	4
2 tbsp	**olive oil**	30 mL
2 tbsp	**lemon juice**	30 mL
1 tbsp	**honey Dijon** **mustard** or (15 mL) Dijon mixed with 1 tsp (5 mL) honey	1 tbsp
2	**garlic cloves** minced	2
1/4 cup	**fresh basil** chopped	60 mL
	salt and pepper, to taste	

Salmon Teriyaki

Salmon Teriyaki

Heat brown sugar, soy sauce, water and lemon juice in a frying pan large enough to hold the salmon snugly. Boil uncovered, stirring occasionally, until sugar is melted. Add salmon, reduce heat and cover. Simmer salmon for 5 to 6 minutes per side. Remove the salmon and keep warm. Boil the sauce until thickened, about 4 minutes. Serve the salmon drizzled with sauce and garnish with lemon slices.

Barbecue
Prepare sauce as directed above. Marinate salmon in sauce for 10 minutes. Preheat the barbecue and oil the grill to minimize sticking. Place on the hot grill and cook over medium-high heat for about 5 minutes per side or until the salmon flakes easily.

SERVES 4

1-1/2 lbs	**salmon fillets or 4 salmon steaks**	681 g
1/2 cup	**brown sugar**	125 mL
1/4 cup	**soy sauce**	60 mL
1/4 cup	**water**	60 mL
2 tbsp	**lemon juice**	30 mL

Indian Yogurt Marinated Salmon

Blend all marinade ingredients. Pour over salmon placed in a zip-locked bag and marinate for at least two hours before cooking. Drain marinade and grill salmon 5 minutes on each side or to desired doneness.

SERVES 4 – 6

4-6	**salmon steaks**	4-6

MARINADE

1 cup	**plain nonfat yogurt**	250 mL
1	**small red onion** chopped	1
2	**garlic cloves** minced	2
1 tbsp	**crystallized ginger** minced	15 mL
1-1/2 tsp	**ground cumin**	7 mL
1 tsp	**nutmeg**	5 mL
1 tsp	**chili powder**	5 mL
1/2 tsp	**fresh ground black pepper**	2 mL
1/2 tsp	**cinnamon**	2 mL
1/4 tsp	**ground cloves**	1 mL
1/4 tsp	**ground cardamom**	1 mL

Smoked Salmon with Smoked Apple Coulis

SERVES 4

1 lb	**salmon fillet**	454 g
1 tsp	**oil**	5 mL
4	**red delicious apples**	4
4 tbsp	**brown sugar**	60 mL
1 tbsp	**coarse salt**	15 mL
1 tbsp	**honey**	15 mL
1 tbsp	**butter**	15 mL
1 tsp	**sweet hot mustard**	5 mL
1/8 tsp	**chili powder**	0.5 mL
1/8 tsp	**salt**	0.5 mL
1/2 cup	**white wine**	125 mL
2 tbsp	**chives** chopped	30 mL

Prepare smoker with hickory wood chips. Heat to 225–250°F (110–120°C). Rub skin of apples with oil and place on smoker rack for 50 to 60 minutes, until soft. Cool.

While apples are smoking, mix brown sugar and salt. Coat both sides of fillet and place it in glass or plastic dish, cover and refrigerate for 30 to 60 minutes (maximum). Rinse the sugar and salt from salmon fillet, pat dry. Place on smoker rack and smoke at 250°F (120°C) degrees for 20 minutes until cooked through.

When apples are cool enough to handle, cut in half, core and scrape apple flesh from skin; discard skin. In a saucepan, mix apple with honey, butter, mustard, chili powder, salt and wine. Heat on medium, stirring to combine. Remove from heat. Using hand blender, blend until smooth. Keep warm. Serve the salmon with smoked apple coulis, and scatter chives on top.

Broiled Salmon with Black Bean Sauce

SERVES 6

6	**salmon steaks** 1-inch thickness	6
2 tbsp	**spicy black bean paste**	30 mL
2 tbsp	**grated fresh ginger**	30 mL
2	**garlic cloves** minced	2
2 tsp	**olive oil**	10 mL
1/2 cup	**red wine**	125 mL
1 tsp	**butter**	5 mL
salt and ground pepper, to taste		

In a small saucepan, whisk together the bean paste, ginger, garlic, olive oil and wine; bring to a boil, lower heat and simmer for 5 minutes, reserve. Butter a broil pan; season both sides of salmon with salt and pepper and place on pan. Brush steaks with reserved bean sauce and broil for 5 minutes, brushing with more sauce frequently. Turn salmon steaks over and repeat process, broiling salmon for another 5 minutes or until salmon flakes easily when pressed with a fork.

Smothered Salmon

In a large frying pan, sauté shrimp and scallops in 2 tablespoons (30 mL) olive oil for 3 minutes or until cooked thoroughly. Remove the cooked shrimp and scallops with a slotted spoon, reserving the oil in the pan. Dice the shrimp (save 4 to 8 whole shrimp to use as a garnish). Sauté onion and garlic in the shrimp oil for 5 minutes; add the peppers, tomato, spices and wine. Cook over medium heat until wine is reduced by half, approximately 10 minutes.

Season the salmon lightly with salt and pepper. Add to the pan, along with the scallops and diced shrimp. Cover and cook on medium-low heat for 3 minutes. Turn and cook an additional 3 minutes. Serve with hot wild rice. Garnish with whole shrimp.

SERVES 4

4 - 4oz	**salmon fillets**	4 - 125 g
1/2 lb	**shrimp** peeled and deveined	227 g
1/2 lb	**scallops** quartered	227 g
2 tbsp	**olive oil**	30 mL
1/2 cup	**diced onion**	125 mL
2	**garlic cloves** chopped	2
3	**hot peppers** diced cayenne, Serrano, red hot and cherry	3
2	**mild peppers** diced, banana or sweet cherry	2
2	**ripe Roma tomatoes** diced	2
1 tbsp	**fresh oregano**	15 mL
1 tbsp	**fresh tarragon**	15 mL
1 tsp	**lemon pepper**	5 mL
1/2 cup	**Chardonnay** dry white wine	125 mL

Cortina Inn & Resort — Chef Keith Paquin's Salmon with Mango Papaya Salsa

Combine all salsa ingredients and adjust seasoning. Grill salmon fillet and serve over greens that have been tossed in a vinaigrette. Top with salsa.

SERVES 1

6 oz	**salmon fillet** seasoned with basil, garlic	170 g
	salt and pepper, to taste	
SALSA		
1	**mango** chopped	1
1	**papaya** chopped	1
1	**juice of a lime**	1
1/2	**red onion** chopped	1/2
	garlic, to taste	
	cumin, to taste	
	salt and pepper, to taste	
1 tbsp	**cilantro** chopped	15 mL

Barbecued Salmon with Blueberry Salsa

Cut salmon into 4 serving portions. Prepare the barbecue and oil the grill. Barbecue salmon skin side down over medium high heat for about 10 minutes per inch of thickness. Spoon salsa over salmon or serve on the side.

SERVES 4

1-1/2 lb	**salmon fillet**	681 g

BLUEBERRY SALSA
Combine just before serving

1/2	**large pink grapefruit** diced sectioned with membrane removed	1/2
2 tbsp	**red onion** finely chopped	30 mL
1	**jalapeno pepper** chopped	1
1 tsp	**honey**	5 mL
1 tbsp	**lime juice**	15 mL
1 cup	**blueberries** fresh or thawed	250 mL
2 tbsp	**fresh cilantro** chopped	30 mL
	salt and pepper to taste	

Alaska Salmon with Nectarine Salsa

Prepare an indirect hot fire in a charcoal or gas grill (prepared according to the manufacturer's directions).

Wash and dry the whole salmon, inside and out. Leave the skin and scales in place to help with handling the cooked fish and to retain the juices. Season the cavity with salt and pepper. Fill the cavity with the sliced lemon, onion and tarragon sprigs. Cut a piece of heavy aluminum foil to the length of the whole salmon. Poke holes at intervals to allow drainage, and spray lightly with cooking oil or butter. Transfer the whole salmon to the foil. Cook indirectly on the preheated grill.

Another option is to lightly smoke the whole salmon, with apple twigs or chips during the cooking process. Cook salmon to desired doneness. Salmon will continue to cook after removing it to platter. Unwrap from foil and serve with salsa.

Nectarine Salsa

Combine nectarine salsa ingredients in a medium-sized bowl. Allow about an hour for the flavors to blend. Serve the nectarine salsa as a condiment. Fresh pineapple, mango or papaya can be substituted for the nectarine.

Salmon

Cook a whole salmon whenever possible. For smaller groups, salmon steaks can be used. Season the salmon steaks with salt, pepper and a little lemon juice. Spread both sides with Dijon style mustard. Grill directly on a bed of tarragon sprigs until done. Cook salmon to desired doneness. Salmon will continue to cook after removing it to platter. Unwrap from foil. Serve with Nectarine Salsa.

SERVES 6 – 8

ALASKA SALMON

1	**whole salmon** cleaned, skin on	1
1	**lemon** sliced thin	1
1	**onion** sliced thin	1
	sprigs of fresh tarragon or dill	
	cooking spray or butter	
	Dijon mustard	

NECTARINE SALSA

1	**medium nectarine** not fully ripe, roughly chopped	1
1	**medium ripe tomato** roughly chopped	1
1/4 cup	**sweet pepper** chopped fine	60 mL
1	**green onion** chopped fine	1
	salt and pepper, to taste	
2 tbsp	**parsley** finely chopped	30 mL
1/8 tsp	**sugar**	0.5 mL
1/8 tsp	**Chinese hot pepper oil**	0.5 mL
1 tsp	**lemon juice**	5 mL

Oasis Ranch Salmon

SERVES 4 – 6

2-1/2 lb	**piece of salmon**	1135 g
1/2 cup	**sun-dried tomatoes in olive oil**	125 mL
2 tsp	**lemon juice**	10 mL
1 tsp	**fresh or dried basil**	5 mL
1 tsp	**fresh or dried dill**	5 mL

Cut salmon into fillets and place in a glass baking dish that has been coated with cooking spray. Spread the sun-dried tomatoes evenly over the fillets. Sprinkle with lemon juice, basil and dill. Bake in a preheated oven at 350°F (175°C) for 10 minutes. Turn oven to low broil and broil for additional 5 minutes on each side.

Thai-style Salmon in Red Curry

SERVES 3

1-1/2 lbs	**salmon fillets** skin on, cut on the bias into 1/2-inch-thick slices	681 g
1 tbsp	**vegetable oil**	15 mL
1 tbsp	**chopped shallots or green onions**	15 mL
1	**Japanese eggplant** halved lengthwise, then cut into 1/2-inch slices	1
2 tbsp	**red curry paste**	30 mL
2 tsp	**fresh ginger** minced	10 mL
1	**can coconut milk** 13.5 fl oz (400 mL)	1
2 tbsp	**fish sauce** nam pla, or to taste	30 mL
1 tbsp	**sugar** or to taste	15 mL
1	**red or yellow sweet pepper** julienned	1
4	**Kaffir lime leaves** very thinly sliced	4
8-10	**Thai basil leaves** coarsely chopped	8-10

Thai basil leaves, coconut milk, red curry paste, and Kaffir lime leaves are available at Asian markets or the specialty food section of most supermarkets. Substitute zest of a lime for Kaffir lime leaves if necessary.

Heat a large heavy skillet or wok over medium-high heat. Add oil, shallots and eggplant and stir-fry until golden, about 2 minutes. Remove and set aside. Add curry paste, ginger and coconut milk to skillet, stir and bring to a boil for 1 minute. Season with fish sauce and sugar. Reduce heat to medium, add eggplant mixture and peppers; cover and simmer for 2 minutes or until eggplant and peppers are tender. Add salmon and cook for 3 to 4 minutes or until salmon just flakes when pressed with a fork. Be careful not to overcook. Add Kaffir lime leaves and Thai basil; and gently stir to mix well. Serve immediately with steamed rice or cooked rice noodles.

Baked Salmon Steaks with Ginger Ratatouille

Preheat oven to 350°F (175°C). In a large skillet, heat oil over medium-high heat; add onion, garlic, ginger and cook, stirring until onions are soft. Add the eggplant, zucchini and peppers, lower heat and cook gently for another 7 to 8 minutes until vegetables are just tender; stir in tomatoes, season with salt and pepper, set aside.

Butter a shallow baking dish and place salmon steaks so they are not touching, pour lemon juice over salmon. Spoon reserved ratatouille over and around the salmon steaks; cover dish tightly with foil. Bake for 20 minutes or until salmon flakes easily when pressed with a fork. Garnish with parsley.

SERVES 4

RATATOUILLE

1 tbsp	**olive oil**	15 mL
1	**small onion** sliced thinly	1
2	**garlic cloves** minced	2
2 tbsp	**fresh ginger** finely chopped	30 mL
1/2 cup	**eggplant** diced	125 mL
1/2 cup	**zucchini**	125 mL
1/2 cup	**red pepper**	125 mL
1	**large tomato** seeded, diced	1
salt and ground pepper, to taste		

SALMON

1 tsp	**butter**	5 mL
4	**salmon steaks** 1-inch thick	4
2 tsp	**fresh lemon juice**	10 mL
2 tbsp	**fresh parsley** chopped	30 mL

YIELD 1/2 cup

6	**egg yolks**	6
1/2 cup	**fish stock**	125 mL
2 tbsp	**Wallace Whisky**	30 mL
6 tbsp	**crème fraiche** or whipping cream	90 mL
1/2 lb	**cold butter** cut into cubes	227 g
	salt, to taste	
	pinch of cayenne pepper	

The Wallace Whisky Sauce for Grilled Salmon

In a heavy saucepan, whisk the egg yolks with the crème fraiche, (or whipping cream), butter, whisky and fish stock over a low heat, to prevent curdling, until the sauce is thick enough to coat the back of a spoon, about 5 minutes. (This sauce will curdle if it gets too hot.) Take it from the heat and season with salt and cayenne pepper.

YIELD 1 1/4 cups

1 cup	**sour cream**	250 mL
1 tsp	**seasoned salt**	5 mL
1/4 tsp	**paprika**	1 mL
2 tsp	**lemon juice**	10 mL
2 tbsp	**prepared horseradish**	30 mL
1 tbsp	**onion** minced	15 mL

Horseradish Sauce for Seafood

Combine all of the ingredients in bowl, whisk for 2 minutes and chill.

YIELD 10 cups

3 cups	**fresh apple juice**	750 mL
4	**Granny Smith apples** sliced	4
4	**Red delicious apples** sliced	4
1	**celery root** cut into matchsticks	1
4 cups	**assorted mushrooms**	1000 mL
1/2 tsp	**parsley**	2mL
1/2 tsp	**chives**	2mL
1/2 tsp	**thyme**	2mL
1/2 tsp	**chervil**	2mL
2 tbsp	**olive oil**	30 mL
2 tbsp	**butter**	30 mL
2	**carrots** sliced thinly	2
	salt and pepper, to taste	

Red & Green Apple Fish Side Dish

Preheat sauté pan with olive oil. Sauté celery root until light golden; add mushrooms, salt and pepper, apples and juice. Add herbs; warm through 2 minutes. Blanch carrots and submerge in cold water. Drain carrots and add to sauté pan. Sprinkle herbs and finish by adding butter. Serve as a side dish to any fish.

Lime Yogurt Salmon Sauce

Combine all ingredients. Coat salmon with yogurt sauce and grill.

YIELD 2/3 cup		
1/2 cup	**plain yogurt**	125 mL
1-1/2 tsp	**fresh chives** chopped	7 mL
1/2 tsp	**fresh parsley** chopped	2 mL
1/2 tsp	**lime peel** minced	2 mL
1/2 tsp	**fresh lime juice**	2 mL
	salt and pepper, to taste	

Elegant Salmon Sauce

Over low heat, place butter in sauté pan. Add onion and sauté gently. Add wine and reduce to half the liquid. Add heavy cream and fresh dill; remove from heat. Serve as condiment with salmon.

YIELD 1 1/4 cups		
2 tbsp	**butter**	30 mL
1/2	**onion** finely chopped	1/2
2 tbsp	**white wine**	30 mL
1 cup	**whipping cream**	250 mL
1 tbsp	**fresh dill**	15 mL

Chilled Sauce for Salmon

Combine ingredients, whisk until well blended. Chill in refrigerator.

YIELD 1/2 cup		
1/2 cup	**sour cream**	125 mL
1 tsp	**prepared horseradish**	5 mL
1/4 tsp	**salt**	1 mL
1/4 tsp	**sugar**	1 mL

Aloha Huelo Point Lookout Lime Ginger Sauce

Combine all ingredients in small saucepan, heat and serve over steamed salmon or white fish.

YIELD 2 cups		
3/4 cup	**dry white wine**	175 mL
2 tsp	**fresh ginger** minced	10 mL
1/2 cup	**whipping cream**	125 mL
1 cup	**unsalted butter** cold, cut up	250 mL
1	**juice of a lime**	1
	salt and pepper, to taste	

YIELD 1 1/4 cups

1/4 cup	mayonnaise	60 mL
1/2 cup	sour cream	125 mL
1/2 cup	Grand Marnier	125 mL
	smoked salmon for dipping	

Grand Marnier Dipping Sauce

Combine the ingredients. This sauce is beautiful for dipping smoked salmon.

YIELD 2 1/2 cups

1/2 cup	raspberry vinegar	125 mL
1/4 cup	minced shallots	60 mL
1/4 cup	whipping cream	60 mL
1 cup	unsalted butter	250 mL
4 tbsp	raspberry jam	60 mL

Raspberry Beurre Blanc Sauce

Combine shallots and vinegar in small sauté pan. Cook over medium heat and reduce liquid by half. Remove from heat. Add whipping cream and continue cooking, reduce to half. Add butter, whisking until mixture is consistency of light mayonnaise. Whisk in raspberry jam. Serve with salmon at room temperature.

YIELD 2 cups

6 tbsp	white wine vinegar	90 mL
1/4 cup	minced shallots	60 mL
2 tbsp	fresh lime juice	30 mL
1/4 cup	whipping cream	60 mL
1 cup	unsalted butter	250 mL
1	lime peel minced	1

Lime Butter Sauce

Combine shallots, vinegar and lime juice in small sauté pan. Cook over medium heat until liquid is reduced by half. Add cream and continue to reduce liquid by half. Remove from heat. Whisk in butter. Return saucepan to low heat and cook until thickened. Blend in lime peel. Serve with salmon at room temperature.

YIELD 1/2 cup

1/4 cup	butter	60 mL
1/4 cup	lemon juice	60 mL
1/4 tsp	dry rosemary	1 mL
1/4 tsp	thyme or dry tarragon	1 mL

Lemon Butter Baste

Melt butter in a small pan over medium heat. Remove from heat and whisk in remainder of the ingredients. Delicious baste for fish.

Shallot Sauce for Salmon Cakes

In a small skillet, melt butter over medium heat. Add lemon zest and shallots. Sauté until shallots are transparent, about 5 minutes; do not let them brown. Add wine, and bring mixture to a low boil. Stirring frequently, cooking until liquid is reduced by half, about 10 minutes. Add whipping cream, salt and pepper, return to a boil stirring until mixture thickens, about 7 minutes. Keep warm.

YIELD 1 3/4 cups

2 tbsp	**butter**	30 mL
1 cup	**Chardonnay** dry white wine	250 mL
1/4 cup	**shallots** sliced very thin	60 mL
1	**egg yolk** lightly blended	1
1 tsp	**lemon zest**	5 mL
1/2 cup	**whipping cream**	125 mL
	salt and pepper, to taste	

Mustard and Rosemary Sauce

In medium sauté pan, reduce 1 cup (250 mL) of dry white wine. Add chopped shallots and three sprigs of rosemary. When reduced to 3 tablespoons (45 mL), add whipping cream and further reduce to 1/4 cup (125 mL). Whisk in Dijon mustard. Serve over grilled salmon.

YIELD 2 1/4 cups

1 cup	**dry white wine**	250 mL
1 cup	**whipping cream**	250 mL
3 sprigs	**rosemary**	3 sprigs
2 tbsp	**Dijon mustard**	30 mL
	chopped shallots	

Peach Olive Tapenade

Place diced peaches in a small bowl with lime juice. Add olives, capers and anchovy paste; stir to combine and set aside. Serve Peach Olive Tapenade with grilled salmon.

SERVES 4

2	**large peaches** peeled, diced in 1/2-inch pieces	2
2 tsp	**lime juice**	10 mL
1/2 cup	**black olives** finely chopped	125 mL
1/4 cup	**pimento-stuffed green olive** finely chopped	60 mL
1 tsp	**capers** drained	5 mL
1	**small can anchovy fillets** minced into a paste	1

The Old Yacht Club Inn Raspberry Beurre Blanc Sauce

YIELD 3 1/2 cups		
2	**shallots** finely diced	2
1 cup	**white wine**	250 mL
2	**sprigs fresh dill** **or tarragon** or 1/2 tsp (2 mL) dried dill weed or tarragon	2
1 cup	**crème fraiche** **or whipping cream**	250 mL
2 tbsp	**seedless** **raspberry jam**	30 mL
1/2 lb	**unsalted butter** cold	227 g
2 cups	**raspberries** fresh or frozen	500 mL
2 tbsp	**fresh dill** **or tarragon** finely chopped or 1 tsp (5 mL) dried dill weed or tarragon	30 mL

Put shallots in heavy saucepan with wine and herbs. Boil over medium heat until the liquid is reduced to 1 tbsp (15 mL) or less. Be careful to avoid boiling dry!

Add crème fraiche or whipping cream and continue to boil to reduce by half. Remove sprigs if you used fresh herbs. Add raspberry jam and whisk into cream mixture. Cut butter into tablespoon-size slices and, over very low heat, whisk the butter into the cream one tablespoon at a time, allowing each slice to melt into the sauce. Continue until all butter is incorporated into sauce. Add half of the raspberries and whisk in. Add herbs and whisk in. Keep over very low heat until ready to serve.

(If sauce gets too hot, the butter will start to melt out). If this happens, add 1 tablespoon 15 mL) of cold butter and whisk in to rebind sauce. Just before serving, add remaining raspberries and gently stir in. serve over salmon or any firm white fish. Yum!

Lemon Sherry Butter Baste

YIELD 2 1/4 cups		
1/4 cup	**butter**	60 mL
1/4 cup	**dry sherry** **or vermouth**	60 mL
1/4 tsp	**dry rosemary**	1 mL
1/4 tsp	**thyme**	1 mL

Melt butter in a small pan over medium heat. Remove from heat and whisk in remaining ingredients. Another delicious baste for fish.

Smoking fish

Any fish can be smoked, but species high in fat (oil) such as salmon and trout are recommended because they absorb smoke faster and have better texture than lean fish, which tend to be dry and tough after smoking.

Use seasoned non-resinous woods: hickory, oak, apple, maple, birch, beech or alder. Avoid pine, fir, spruce, etc. or green woods. If heavier smoke flavor is desired, add moist sawdust to the heat source throughout the smoking process.

Control heat by adjusting airflow.

Control temperature
Hot-smoking: 90°F for the first 2 hours; 150°F for remaining smoking time.

Cold-smoking: 80–90°F for 1–5 days or more

Lox: 70–80°F for 1–3 days

Preparing Fish for Smoking
Use only freshly-caught fish that have been kept clean and cold. Fish that have been handled carelessly or stored under improper conditions will not produce a satisfactory finished product. Do not use bruised, broken, or otherwise damaged flesh.

If you catch your fish, clean and pack them in ice before starting home. When you get home, store the fish in the refrigerator until you are ready to prepare them for smoking.

Different fish species generally require specific preparation methods. Salmon are split (backbone removed); bottom fish are filleted; herring are headed and gutted, and smelt are dressed. The following preparation steps can be applied to any fish:

1 Remove scales by scraping against the grain with the dull edge of a knife.

2 Remove head, fins, tail, viscera.

3 Wash body cavity with running cold water to remove all traces of blood and kidney tissue (dark red mass along the backbone).

4 Split the fish by cutting through the rib bones along the length of one side of the backbone.

5 For large fish, remove the backbone by cutting along the other side of the backbone to produce two fillets or boneless sides. For small fish, the backbone can be left attached to one of the sides.

6 Cut the sides of large fish into uniform pieces about 1-1/2 inches thick and 2 inches wide. Small fish halves can be brined and smoked in one piece.

Smoking fish

Preparing brine

Prepare a brine of 3-1/2 cups table salt in 1 gallon of cold water in a plastic, stainless steel or crockery container. Red or white wine can be substituted for a portion or all of the water, if desired. Stir the salt until a saturated solution is formed.

Spices such as black pepper, bay leaves, seafood seasoning, or garlic, as well as brown sugar, may be added to the brine depending on your preference.

Use 1 gallon of brine for every 4 pounds of fish. Brine fish in the refrigerator, if possible.

Keep the fish covered with brine throughout the brining period. A heavy bowl can be floated on the brine to keep the fish submersed, but do not pack the fish so tightly that the brine cannot circulate around each piece.

Cold smoking

1 To cold-smoke fish, follow steps 1–6 under "Preparing Fish For Smoking".

2 Brine 1/2-inch-thick fillets for 1/2 hour; 1-inch-thick fillets for 1 hour, and 1 1/2-inch-thick fillets for 2 hours. Brining times can be lengthened if the cold-smoked fish are to be preserved for long periods of time.

3 After brining, rinse the fish briefly in cold running water.

4 Place the fish skin-side down on greased racks in a cool shady, breezy place to dry. The fish should dry for 2 to 3 hours or until a shiny skin or pellicle has formed on the surface. A fan will speed pellicle formation.

5 Place the fish in a homemade or commercial smoker. The temperature of the smoker should be kept at about 80°F, and should never exceed 90°F. If a thermometer is not available, the temperature may be tested by hand. If the air in the smokehouse feels distinctly warm, the temperature is too high.

6 Smoke the fish until its surface is an even brown. Small fish that are to be kept 2 weeks or less may be ready in 24 hours. Salmon and other large fish will require 3 to 4 days and nights of steady smoking. To store longer than 2 weeks, smoke all fish a minimum of five days; for larger fish, at least a week or longer.

7 The smoker should not produce a lot of smoke during the first 8 to 12 hours if the total curing time is 24 hours, or for the first 24 hours if the curing time is longer. When the first part of the smoking ends, build up a dense smoke and maintain it for the balance of the cure.

8 If cold-smoked fish has been brined for at least 2 hours and smoked for at least 5 days, it will keep in the refrigerator for several months.

Smoking fish

Hot smoking

1 To hot-smoke fish, follow steps 1–6 under "Preparing Fish for Smoking."

2 Brine 1/2-inch-thick fillets for about 15 minutes, 1-inch-thick pieces about 30 minutes, and 1-1/2-inch-thick pieces about 1 hour. Brining times can be adjusted to give the fish a lighter or heavier cure.

3 After brining, rinse the fish briefly in cold running water.

4 Place the fish skin-side down on greased racks in a cool, shady, breezy place to dry. The fish should dry for 2 to 3 hours or until a shiny skin or pellicle forms on the surface. The pellicle seals the surface and prevents loss of natural juices during smoking. A fan will speed pellicle formation.

5 Place the fish in a homemade or commercial smoker. For the first 2 hours, the temperature should not exceed 90°F. This completes the pellicle formation and develops brown coloring.

6 After the initial 2-hour period, raise the temperature to 150°F and smoke the fish for an additional 4 to 8 hours. The length of time will depend on the thickness of the fish, and on your preference for dry or moist smoked fish. Generally, 1/2-inch-thick pieces are smoked for 4 hours, 1-inch-thick pieces for 6 hours, and 1-1/2-inch-thick pieces for 8 hours.

7 Store hot-smoked fish in the refrigerator.

Tips on grilling seafood

1 A hinged wire grill basket is best for cooking whole fish such as salmon. It also works well for fillets of tender fish such as perch, snapper, catfish or flounder.

2 Firm fish, such as salmon, can be cooked directly on the grill if handled carefully.

3 Grill fillets over medium to medium-low heat. Fish can cook quickly and it is easier to slow down cook time and monitor to not over cook.

4 Turn fish only once. (Flipping back and forth will break fish apart.)

5 If using a marinade, allow fish to soak up flavor for at least 30 minutes. Refrigerate while soaking in marinade.

6 If you are going to use the marinade as an extra sauce on top of the cooked fish, the marinade liquid must be boiled by itself for at least 5 minutes to cook out any bacteria that may be there from when the fish was soaking.

Diamond pattern on grilled fish

1 Prior to starting the grill. Pour a small amount of vegetable oil on a paper towel and lightly coat the grill rack. This will help from having the fish stick to your rack. (If the grill's already started, it's usually too hot to get your hand close enough to do it, plus not too safe with the oil.

2 Preheat the grill to medium-high.

3 Brush or pat both sides of the fish lightly with olive oil.

4 Cook without turning on first side for 2 to 3 minutes.

5 Rotate fish 45-degrees on the grill (a one-quarter turn). Cook for 2 to 3 minutes longer.

6 Flip fish to other side and finish cooking time.

Additional cooking time in the microwave

If you're not sure grilled fish is done, you can cook it in the microwave oven for another minute or two. (This can over cook your fish very quickly and make the fish dry or rubbery textured, so watch the timing).

1 Cook fish for half the required time on a barbecue grill. This gives the fish the attractive grill marks and some grilled flavor.

2 Transfer the fish to a microwave-safe baking dish and cook 1 to 2 minutes to finish cooking the fish. Press or flake with a fork to test for doneness.

3 Remember, fish continues to cook after it is removed from the microwave oven so allow 1 to 2 minutes standing time before you cook it any longer.

How to freeze fish

1 Rinse under cold, running water until water runs clear. Pat dry with paper towels. Wrap tightly in plastic wrap, squeezing out all the air.

2 Wrap again in aluminum foil.

3 Write contents and date on a freezer label or strip of making tape.

4 Freeze as quickly as possible.

5 For best results, thaw and use within two weeks.

Credits

It is not without help and encouragement that one is able to even begin the publication of a book. I would like to recognize all of those very special people that have supported me on "The Salmon Cookbook". These people have been dedicated to providing me with the best of the best recipes and photograps to help make this Salmon Cookbook a best seller.
I deeply appreciate their help and understanding with this project.

Photo Credits

British Columbia
Salmon Marketing Council
Donald Grant Snell

California Salmon Council
David Goldenberg

Sandy Krogh, Culinary Consultant
for her ongoing support for the wish list.

Credits

7 Gables Inn, Fairbanks, Alaska

The 1785 Inn Bed & Breakfast and Restaurant, North Conway, New Hampshire

1794 Watchtide By The Sea Searsport, Maine

Abigail's Elegant Victorian Mansion, Victoria British Columbia

Alaska Seafood Council

Aloha Huelo Point Lookout Huelo, Maui, Hawaii

Anchorage Mahogany Manor, Historic Downtown Inn Anchorage, Alaska

The Apricot Cat Vancouver, British Columbia

Blue Heron Glacier Bay Bed & Breakfast Gustavus, Alaska

Café Valdez, Valdez Alaska

Carter House Victorians Eureka, California

Casa de La Paz Bayfront St. Augustine, Florida

Cascade View Bed & Breakfast Bellevue, Washington

Chef Ray, Loon River Café

Chef June

Chef Tim Schafer

Cortina Inn & Resort Killington, Vermont

Crystal Palace, Bristol, Vermont

Dekoven Suites, Brooklyn, New York

The Eighteenth Street Inn Bed & Breakfast Fort Lauderdale, Florida

Fish 4 Fun

Flery Manor, Grants Pass, Oregon

Gunflint Lodge, Grand Marais, Minnesota

Hartness House Inn, Bed and Breakfast & Restaurant, Springfield, Vermount

Inn at Portsmouth Harbor Kittery, Maine

Kedron Valley Inn, South Woodstock, Vermont

The Lilac Inn Bed & Breakfast and Restaurant, Brandon, Vermont

The Mill House Inn East Hampton, Long Island, New York

Mountain View, Indian Hills, Colorado

North Atlantic Fisheries College Shetland Salmon Farmers' Association

The Oasis Ranch, Skull Valley, Arizona

Old Town Inn, Eureka, California

The Old Yacht Club Inn Santa Barbara, California

The Painted Lady, Elmira, New York

The Seal Beach Inn and Gardens Seal Beach, California

Index

A

Abigail's Elegant Victorian Mansion Creamed Eggs with Smoked Salmon in Puff Pastry, 30

Abigail's Hotel Smoked Salmon Scrambled Eggs, 39

Asian Style Steamed Salmon, 59

Alaska Salmon with Nectarine Salsa, 81

Alaska Sockeye Salmon Strudel, 74

Aloha Huelo Point Lookout Lime Ginger Sauce, 85

B

Baked Salmon Steaks with Ginger Ratatouille, 83

Barbecued Salmon with Blueberry Salsa, 80

Barbecued Salmon Burgers, 74

Blue Heron Glacier Bay Smoked Omelet, 30

Braised Salmon and Fennel, 72

Broiled Salmon with Black Bean Sauce, 78

C

Café Valdez Classic Salmon Chowder, 20

Fresh Poached Salmon Salad with Fruit and Raspberry-Orange Vinaigrette, 25

King Salmon in Silver Packets, 12

King Salmon Wrap Appetizers, 9

King Salmon Fillets with Country Herb Crust, 70

Cascade View Bagels and Lox Benedict, 31

Casa de La Paz Bayfront Smoked Salmon Tart, 31

Cedar Plank Salmon, 46

Chef June's Salmon Guadalupe, 69

Chilled Sauce for Salmon, 85

Chili Grilled Salmon with Mango Salsa, 35

Cooking Tips

    Additional cooking time in the microwave, 92

    Diamond pattern on grilled fish, 92

    Grilled seafood 91

    How to freeze fish, 92

    Smoking fish, 89

Cortina Inn and Resort – Chef Keith Paquin's Salmon with Mango Papaya Salsa, 79

Cream of Salmon Soup, 20

Crystal Palace Poached Salmon, 48

E

Easy Hollandaise Sauce, 40

Elegant Salmon Sauce, 85

F

Flery Manor "Between the Sheets", 36

French Scrambled Eggs with Smoked Salmon, 38

Fresh Alaska Salmon Italian Bread Salad, 24

G

7 Gables Inn Broccoli Salmon Quiche, 13

Ginger-Sesame Salmon, 57

Gold Medal Grilled Tequila Salmon, 48

Grand Marnier Dipping Sauce, 86

Grilled Salmon Sandwich with Roasted Summer Vegetables, 42

Grilled Salmon with Ginger Butter, 67

Grilled Wild King Salmon Skewers with Gazpacho Salsa, 10

Index

H

Hartness House Hazelnut Braised Salmon, 52
Honey bourbon Salmon, 46
Honey Lime BBQ Kebobs, 50
Honey Mustard Basil Salmon, 75
Horseradish Sauce for Seafood, 84

I

Inn at Portmouth Harbor Corn Cakes with Smoked Salmon and Crème Fraiche, 55
Indian Yogurt Marinated Salmon, 77

K

Kedron Valley Inn Smoked Salmon Parfait with Parmesan Toast, 15
"Kings" King Salmon and Cognac Spread, 14

L

Lemon Butter Baste, 86
Lemon Grass and Apricot Stuffed BBQ Salmon, 57
Lemon Sherry Butter Baste, 88
Lime Butter Sauce, 86
Lime Grilled Salmon Steaks with Tomato Avocado Salsa, 73
Lime Yogurt Salmon Sauce, 85
Loon River Café Salmon Stew, 26

M

Mahogany Glazed Salmon, 49
Mahogany Manor Golden Baked Salmon with Blueberry Salsa, 59
Maple Mango-Tango Salmon, 75

Market Sauté of Salmon, 39
Mediterranean Salmon, 65
Minted Salmon and Asparagus Stir Fry, 63
Mountain View Fatad with Smoked Salmon, 41
Mustard and Rosemary Sauce, 87
My Sister Louise's Teriyaki Salmon Steaks, 54

O

Oasis Ranch Salmon, 60
Old Town Inn Dilled Eggs with Smoked Salmon, 38

P

Pasta with Asparagus and Smoked Salmon, 33
Peach Olive Tapenade, 87
Peking Salmon, 49
Pacific Ocean Salmon with Fresh Vegetables and Herbs, 62

R

Ranchero Grilled Salmon Steak with Roasted Corn-Black Bean Salsa, 64
Raspberry Beurre Blanc Sauce, 86
Red & Green Apple Fish Side Dish, 84
Roasted Salmon Mediterranean, 54

S

Salad
California Fresh Poached Salmon Salad with Fruit and Raspberry-Orange Vinaigrette, 25
Fresh Alaska Salmon Italian Bread Salad, 24

Index

Summer Tomato Salad, 19

Wildwood Herbed Baked Salmon on Rock Salt with Late Summer Tomato Salad, 19

Salmon and Crab Bisque, 21

Salmon and Cucumber Salad, 21

Salmon Soup, 26

Salmon Steaks with Dill Butter, 61

Salmon Steaks with Spinach Pesto, 52

Salmon Steaks with Vermouth, 56

Salmon Teriyaki, 77

Salmon with Basil & Champagne Cream Sauce, 56

Salmon with Crab Sauce, 51

Salmon with Lime Yogurt Sauce, 66

Seared Salmon with Caramelized Onions, 51

Shallot Sauce for Salmon Cakes, 87

Simple Salmon Salad, 23

Smoked Salmon and Fennel Potato Pizza, 41

Smoked Salmon and Chevre Cheesecake, 8

Smoked Salmon Stuffed Cucumber Slices, 8

Smoked Salmon with Smoked Apple Coulis, 78

Smoked Salmon Roll Ups, 15

Smoked Salmon Wraps and Salad, 40

Smoked! Fire! and Ice! Alaska Salmon Steaks, 61

Smothered Alaskan Salmon, 79

Soup

    Café Valdez Classic Salmon Chowder, 20

    Salmon and Crab Bisque, 21

    Salmon Soup, 26

T

Thai-style Salmon in Red Curry, 60

The 1785 Inn Smoked Salmon Raviolis Pasta, 68

The Apricot Cat BBQ Salmon Strata, 37

The Eighteenth Street Inn Rubbed and Roasted Salmon, 72

The Lilac Inn Smoked Salmon Quesadilla, 37

The Mill House Inn Smoked and Cream Cheese Quesadillas, 32

The Old Yacht Club Inn Raspberry Beurre Blanc Sauce, 88

The Painted Lady Smoked Salmon Roulade, 43

The Seal Beach Inn Curry Salmon Quiche, 33

The Wallace Whisky Sauce for Grilled Salmon, 84

U

Umberto's "Salmone Fresco Marinato", 71

V

Vermouth Salmon, 71

W

1794 Watchtide by The Sea Smoked Salmon Claffouti, 32

Wildwood Herbed Baked Salmon on Rock Salt with Late Tomato Salad, 19

Wildwood Wild Salmon Cakes, 23

Y

Yoo-Sah or Sockeye Mulligan Stew, 35

Z

Zesty Salmon Steaks, 66